THE MEANING OF BALANCE SHEETS
AND COMPANY REPORTS

a guide for non-accountants

L. E. ROCKLEY, BCom(Lond), MPhil(Warwick), IPFA, AMBIM
Principal Lecturer, Lanchester Polytechnic, Coventry

The Meaning of Balance Sheets and Company Reports

a guide for non-accountants

BUSINESS BOOKS

London   Melbourne   Sydney   Auckland   Johannesburg

Business Books Ltd

An imprint of the Hutchinson Publishing Group

17–21 Conway Street, London W1P 5HL

Hutchinson Group (Australia) Pty Ltd
30–32 Cremorne Street, Richmond South, Victoria 3121
PO Box 151, Broadway, New South Wales 2007

Hutchinson Group (NZ) Ltd
32–34 View Road, PO Box 40–086, Glenfield, Auckland 10

Hutchinson Group (SA) (Pty) Ltd
PO Box 337, Bergvlei 2012, South Africa

First published 1975
Reprinted 1977, 1981

© Lawrence Edwin Rockley 1975

Printed in Great Britain by The Anchor Press Ltd
and bound by Wm Brendon & Son Ltd
both of Tiptree, Essex

ISBN 0 220 66276 2

TO MARGARET, AGAIN

Contents

Objects of the balance sheet — Value in use of corporate
assets: resources employed, capital invested and the
relevance of asset valuations — Proprietors' ownership-
net worth — Classification of items in the balance sheet
— Fixed assets and the concept of depreciation: revaluation of fixed assets — Investments: interest in
subsidiaries — Current assets: valuation of stock and
work in progress — Capital expenses —Authorised and
issued capital: classes of Preference share: reserves: loan
stock — Current liabilities — Flow of funds

Narrative and consolidated balance sheets — Information accompanying published accounts: statement of movements of fixed assets — Capital employed and capital invested: shareholders' capital employed: the deferred taxation account: net asset value of an ordinary share — Working capital: current and liquid ratios: appraising liquidity states — Relationships between fixed interest/dividend capital and equity — Conditions for issue of debentures: effects of gearing: corporate cost of capital

The profit and loss account: form and content — Receipts and payments: income and expenditure — Gross and net cash flows: the depreciation charge — Funds Flow Statements: comparative balance sheet analysis: financing strategies: working capital flow — Cash flows from published accounts. Appraising the adequacy of cash flows: future capital expenditure

Return on capital employed — Consequences of historic cost accounting — Fall in value of the monetary unit and the appropriateness of asset book values — Choosing alternative appraisal criteria — Anatomy of the return on capital ratio — Working capital management — Earnings per share and market worth of Ordinary shares: earnings yield: dividend, dividend yield and dividend cover — Post-tax earnings under imputation: nil, net and actual earnings — Preference shares: loan stock: priority percentages

The failures of historic cost recording: revaluation of fixed assets and the impact of subjective opinion — Current purchasing power accounting: currency con-

version indexes: supplementary value adjusted balance
sheets and profit and loss accounts and the continuance
of historic cost based final accounts: company performance and wealth comparisons — Treatment of
fixed assets and calculation of depreciation charges —
Monetary and non-monetary items; the influence of
inflation on holdings of such assets and liabilities —
Examples of inflation adjusted accounts — Profit and
loss accounts and loss of purchasing power from holding
net monetary assets. Published accounts: Currys and
GKN — Alternative methods: replacement cost method
of accounting for fixed assets: writing up fixed assets:
the current value method: the replacement cost method

Preface

The information published in the annual report and accounts booklets of many UK companies is nowadays very detailed and extensive, and can be of considerable value for appraising corporate worth and profitability. But to the non-financial mind this mass of data renders the task of accounts analysis even more daunting: a fact which surely was not the object of our legislators or of the directors of those firms whose published accounts are presented in such informative and well thought out styles.

In writing this book therefore my principal objective has been to show the reader firstly, how the balance sheets and accounts are constructed and secondly, how to use the information reported in those statements — and in the accompanying notes — to evaluate important aspects of business wealth and profitability. Now a realistic study of business financial statements cannot be completed by reference to *hypothetical* examples only. It is in the practical application of book learning that true understanding is tested and refined.

Thus I have been most encouraged by permissions given to me by appropriate officials of the following companies to use data from their annual report and accounts booklets, in writing this book. The reader will gain further benefit from studying the complete booklets of these companies, and watching their progress from year to year:

> Booker McConnell Limited
> Currys Limited
> Courtaulds Limited
> Guest, Keen and Nettlefolds Limited
> Marks & Spencer Limited
> Tesco Stores (Holdings) Limited

I am pleased to acknowledge also the permission given by Her Majesty's Stationery Office to reproduce appropriate data from the Companies Acts. Finally I wish to thank my colleague Mr A. E. W. Laugharne, who read the manuscript on Accounting for Inflation and Disclosure of Information, for his valuable advice and comments. Nevertheless the responsibility for the views, methods and techniques which appear in this book is mine alone.

Kenilworth 1975   L. E. ROCKLEY

Anatomy of the Balance Sheet 1

Introduction

> 'A balance sheet is thus an historic document and does
> not purport to show the net worth of an undertaking at any
> particular date.'

The above quotation is taken from the report on Company Law
Amendment which was issued in 1948 by the Cohen Committee. To
a large extent it holds good today as a description of most corporate
balance sheets. They are merely statements which enumerate the
sources and amounts of money and credit which have been made
available to a firm: they also show what those funds were spent on—
the physical assets. All of these items form a resource picture of the
firm as it existed at a specific time — the date of the balance sheet.
But in most instances the money values given therein to fixed assets
are based upon their initial acquisition costs which were incurred

(possibly) some years ago. This is so despite the fact that their *current* money values may be several times greater than those shown. Such disparaties between the historic and the present money values have arisen mainly as a result of inflation and the consequent fall in the value of money. Other value disparities will have resulted from changes in the technologies of production, and some from the emergence of scarcities. Nevertheless the greatest impact upon resource values has undoubtedly come from the falling value of money.

Thus we need to ask 'What is the object of a balance sheet: what is it expected to show?' There are several answers which could be given to these questions, but two of the most important features of the worthwhileness of corporate final accounts will be explained in order to give some response to the questions about balance sheet rationale.

Firstly, so far as the assets are concerned — and this applies especially to the fixed assets — a balance sheet does not pretend to describe a list of items which are available for sale by the company. If such a sale took place the company would cease to exist! Again, so far as the liabilities are concerned, the statement does not describe a list of debts due for immediate redemption. No, a balance sheet gives data about a firm presently in business, and moreover a firm expecting to continue in business. Continuance in a trading situation implies that the firm will use its physical possessions* and its funds in the pursuit of earning an income. The prime consideration therefore has been the value in use of corporate assets, not their value in exchange. For this reason a balance sheet has never been expected to show the market value of assets recorded therein. Furthermore, liabilities are classified into those repayable in the short term and those repayable in the long term. Some liabilities, such as shares, are repayable in certain special circumstances only.

Resources employed or capital invested

Now, arising from the concept value in use of corporate assets we must recognise that a balance sheet can describe the resources available for employment by the business in its trading operations. The main problem which hinders our effective use of the statement for this purpose, lies in our not achieving up to date realistic values for the various types of asset and the various ages of those assets which are

*No balance sheet contains a complete list of the firm's assets. Goodwill, the skills of its management and its workforce are examples of corporate assets which are never realistically quantitified for inclusion amongst the firm's possessions.

listed in balance sheets. However the problem of asset valuation and its solution in balance sheet terms is not a topic with which to *start* our education in the objects and uses of company final accounts. At this stage the book values (those monetary values shown) of the firm's available resources will form the subject of our study.

When the balance sheet values of resources employed are matched with the value of the outputs produced by those resources, then we can calculate and express in percentage terms an indicator of relative efficiency. That indicator is called 'return on capital employed': with some reservations and modifications it represents a useful measure of overall average efficiency of performance. When the objective of a balance sheet is taken to be a statement of the long term resources invested in the business, then this is how that information can be used.

The second response to the question about the aims of a balance sheet refers to an assessment of the value of the proprietors' (the shareholders) ownership of the firm. Clearly this concept must embrace the difference between

1   The value of the firm's possessions — its assets,
     and
2   The amount of the debts payable to third parties, i.e. other than to the proprietors.

Here we have the notion of a firm's net worth, which was referred to in the quotation from the Cohen Report. It describes the *funds* invested in the firm by the proprietors and consists of monies subscribed for shares in the business plus profits ploughed back, i.e. not issued as dividends to the proprietors.

Business managers, investors and creditors each seek answers to their own questions about a firm's profitability and credit rating. In many instances the final accounts are all that is readily available for such people to use in appraising a company's financial and profit status. The effects of continued inflation upon the reliability of the capital employed and net worth amounts are widely known and appreciated. It would therefore be an over-reaction to this state of affairs to reject balance sheet data entirely, when corporate profitability, liquidity and net worth are to be appraised.

The need to update monetary values accorded to items in the balance sheet is not questioned. If more realistic values can be given to these assets and liabilities then the concepts of capital employed and net worth would be more meaningful. In this matter the writer welcomes the measures being taken to encourage companies to publish final account supplementary statements showing their financial results in terms of pounds of purchasing power at the end of the year to which the accounts relate.* But many of the monetary values shown in the final accounts are influenced by factors other than inflation. The application of certain accounting conventions will determine — in some cases somewhat arbitrarily — the apportionment of costs between one or more operating periods in a firm's life. Cost apportionment problems affect both profit and loss accounts *and* balance sheets. So a clear understanding of the content and purpose of both of these statements is essential if the reader wishes to achieve a better appreciation of a firm's worth in terms of

1   Its physical possessions — assets.
2   Its earning power — the efficiency with which those assets are used.

The balance sheet

The balance sheet is a financial statement: it gives information about a firm's financial position in terms of what it owes and what it owns. These facts are relevant to one point in time only — the date shown in the title heading.

In a sense a balance sheet (see Exhibit 1) fulfils two functions: (a) it records the firm's liability and assets status at the end of a trading period and (b) it forms a starting point for the next trading period in that it shows what is available for the firm's use in that next period. The information link between two successive balance sheets is a profit and loss account. Thus the profit and loss account forms a bridge between two balance sheets and records the operational details of how the firm proceeded from date 1 to date 2.

Now a business is continually on the move. It is daily engaging in transactions which must affect its ownings and owings and therefore the date of the balance sheet is of vital importance. One further day in the life of the firm would produce numerous changes in balance sheet data such as

1   Changes in the figure of debtors — due to additional sales on credit, or to the payment by debtors of amounts due from them.
2   Changes in creditors and stock due to raw materials purchased on credit.

Therefore whenever we appraise the worth of a company — and a balance sheet is one of the statements we would need for such a

*See pages 143-70 for an explanation of the mechanics of accounting for inflation and the presentation of supplementary final account statements which demonstrate the impact of changing money values upon corporate profits and net worth, etc.

Exhibit 1   5

THE GROWING COMPANY LIMITED

Balance Sheet as at 31 December 19..

Entries on this side show where the funds and credit came from – what the company owes at the above date	Entries on this side show how the money was spent – what the company owns at the above date

study — we must be sure that the balance sheet which we have available is an up to date one and is appropriate for the time scale of our study.

Beneath the title heading and in the body of the balance sheet, particulars of the firm's assets will be recorded together with details of the different kinds of finance which were necessary to enable the company to acquire those assets. The information is presented with items of a similar nature being grouped together. The various classifications of a company's assets and liabilities are described by subtitles such as

Fixed Assets
Investments
Current Assets
Issued Capital
Reserves
Loan capital
Current Liabilities

There are good reasons for showing a business' finance and asset structure in this way. A clearer picture of the firm's production capacity (fixed assets) and its capital financing strengths will be given when items of a similar nature and function are brought together. This makes analysis easier for the different people — institutional investors, financial analysts, government statisticians, trade unions, and managers — who are interested in company affairs. Moreover suppliers of materials or components for manufacture and trading will be concerned about the firm's ability to settle its short term debts. Therefore they will look at the amount of *current* liabilities which the firm already owes. These are debts of the current period only and are normally settled within a month or so. They should be compared with that group of the corporate possessions called 'current assets'. These are assets of the current period. They include stocks of raw materials, work-in-progress, finished goods, and debtors — descriptions of items which are being converted into cash. Together with cash, they constitute the fund from which the short term creditors will be paid.

Thus the intending creditor (for supplies) will want to see that the value of the current assets is at least equal to the value of the present current liabilities. More than likely he will prefer that the total value of the current assets amounts to twice that of the current liabilities in order to give sufficient 'cover' for the sums needed to meet the liabilities of the current period. That cover is a safeguard, a form of insurance against any loss in value of some of the current assets through adverse trading conditions or loss of markets. Such techniques and comparisons as are used in appraising a company's worth as it is revealed in the final accounts must await a later chapter. For the moment it is intended to take the reader through a detailed examination of each section of our company's balance sheet. In this way an appropriate knowledge will be secured upon which informed evaluations can be based.

Fixed assets

Fixed assets are the company's capital expenditures. They represent the firm's *past* investment in long-lived assets — physical assets which the firm still possesses and which are expected to continue contributing to its earning power for several years. Such possessions are not held for resale. Therefore they are not shown at resale or market values. Customarily they will appear as in Exhibit 2 below, at the original acquisition cost less accumulated depreciation.

Values given for items in a balance sheet are referred to as the book values. Thus the amount of £175,000 relating to the land and buildings is the book value of those possessions — it is not the market value. The total net book value of the fixed assets, £385,000, is derived from their original acquisition costs £684,000, less the total depreciation to date, £299,000. That depreciation sum represents the proportion of the original costs, which is presumed at the date of the balance sheet to have been 'consumed' by the firm in its past manufacturing and trading operations. It recognises the fact that in the profit and loss accounts relating to *each* of the years during which the firm has possessed the fixed assets, a charge for the use of those assets will have been included amongst the year's operating expenses.

Exhibit 2   7

THE GROWING COMPANY LIMITED

Balance Sheet as at 31 December 19..

	Cost or valuation £	Aggregate depreciation £	£
FIXED ASSETS			
Land and buildings	250,000	75,000	175,000
Plant	358,000	198,000	160,000
Vehicles	60,000	20,000	40,000
Equipment	16,000	6,000	10,000
	£684,000	£299,000	385,000

The summation of the separate annual depreciation charges produces the 'aggregate depreciation' figures given in the balance sheet.

Depreciation is the term used to describe the concept of 'cost of use' of fixed assets: it may be calculated by somewhat unscientific methods.* In fact all that depreciation sets out to do is a spreading of the asset's net acquisition costs — the historical cost less an estimated sales value upon retirement — over the several accounting periods of the asset's economic life.

Clearly the net book values of fixed assets will decline with the passage of each year, as each year's depreciation charge reduces still further the balance sheet values of the assets concerned. However continued inflation and the consequent fall in the value of money must result in some of these assets being worth more today than they originally cost. But if a balance sheet is to be regarded as a statement of resources which the firm needs and uses to earn its income (see pp. 2–3) then it must be desirable that realistic resource values should be used. Therefore corporate assets should be quoted at up-to date values such as are appropriate to the period in which the profit itself was earned.

For this reason some businesses revise the book values of their fixed assets so as to bring them more into line with their present day

*See L.E. Rockley, *Finance for the non-accountant,* pp 18-24, Business Books (Second edition, 1976)

prices. This process is termed revaluing the fixed assets and it requires the kind of descriptive title 'cost or valuation' which is found in Exhibit 2. Where assets are revalued the annual depreciation charges will become allocations of the revalued amounts and will be based upon the increased figures of worth. A greater charge to the profit and loss account will ensue, except when opinions about the asset's expected future life are revised so as to indicate a longer period of effective economic use in the future. From such revisions of asset values and the concomitant depreciation charges we should be able to secure better information about

1 The asset worth of the firm.

2 The current cost of engaging in business and earning profit.

Following upon the recording of more realistic fixed asset values in a balance sheet, the company's power to borrow may be enhanced also. This would result from a greater asset cover being available to act as security for the additional borrowing. Again under-valued assets are frequently a material factor in a take-over situation. Asset revaluations will increase a firm's net worth which would tend to give the firm a higher value in the eyes of the business world. In consequence share prices would tend to rise thus making a take-over bid more costly to the potential bidder. Such share price movements reflect the increased value of the total shareholders' funds — the net worth — for these funds must be augmented by an amount corresponding to the net revaluation increase. A revaluation reserve is created to show the extent to which the proprietors' capital has been amended in this way.

Investments

Exhibit 3 sets out the next group of assets that our company possesses.

Investments which are owned by a manufacturing or trading company, i.e. NOT an investment company, are bought for many reasons. Some, like the fixed assets, are not held primarily for resale. Such investments represent the company's interest in other business houses. These other business houses may be called

1 Associated or affiliated companies — where the Growing Company, for example, does not own a controlling interest in the other company.

2 Subsidiary companies — where the Growing Company, for example, holds more than one half of the nominal value of the equity share capital of the other company.

A substantial equity shareholding in other business concerns may enable the parent company to establish certain trading arrangements expected to be beneficial to its own future development and profitability. In this way, the sources of components and raw materials and perhaps ultimate markets may be secured. Joint schemes of marketing, management and production can be set in train for the good of both companies. Sometimes an existing limited company may wish to develop a new line or a new area of business activity. A subsidiary company can be formed for this special purpose, giving all the benefits of limited liability and ensuring the creation of a fresh corporate image for the new business line.

A company may also own investments which are NOT bought for trade control or joint operation purposes. Shares, loan stock or debentures might be held mainly for the dividends or interest which the owner of such investments would receive. But whatever investments are owned by a company, they must be revealed in its balance sheet as is shown in Exhibit 3. Two principal groups of these assets have to be specified. For investments *other than* those relating to subsidiary companies, the total amount must be divided into 'quoted' and 'unquoted' investments. The sub-classification enables distinction to be made between

1   Those investments which have been granted a quotation or

Exhibit 3

THE GROWING COMPANY LIMITED

Balance Sheet as at 31 December 19..

	£	£
Fixed Assets		385,000
INVESTMENTS		
Quoted (MV £64,000)	50,000	
Unquoted (Directors' valuation £28,000)	25,000	75,000
INTEREST IN SUBSIDIARIES		
Shares	125,000	
Amounts owing by subsidiary	25,000	
	150,000	
Amounts owing to subsidiary	15,000	135,000

permission to deal on a recognised stock exchange — the quoted share or debenture.

2   Those investments where no such quotation or permission has been granted — the unquoted share or debenture.

The distinction is important for the value which investments are shown in the balance sheet will normally be their cost of acquisition. But so far as quoted investments are concerned the balance sheet must show also their aggregate market value (MV) at the date of the balance sheet, if this is different from the book value. Furthermore if the stock exchange value is lower than the above-mentioned market value, then that stock exchange value must be stated.

For the unquoted shares or debentures it is customary for the balance sheet to carry a note of the directors' valuation of the worth of those shares or debentures. To do this avoids (for equity shares) the statutory requirement to give a great deal more information about the unquoted investments. This additional information would have to reveal the

1   Total income received from the investments during the year.

2   Accumulated share of the total undistributed profits (of the companies whose shares are held) which have arisen since acquisition of those shares.

3   The way in which losses, incurred by the companies whose shares are held, have been dealt with in the accounts of the firm to whom the balance sheet relates, e.g. the Growing Company.

Now we have discussed the advisability of revaluing the fixed assets in order to present a more realistic valuation of the resources employed in a business. Yet it would be of little worth to be repeatedly revaluing *investments* according to stock exchange prices at the dates of successive balance sheets. Stock exchange prices fluctuate from day to day. They do not necessarily reflect the underlying strengths or weaknesses, only, of the shares in question. Other influences than inherent commercial profitability have their impact upon the optimism or pessimism of investors, and hence upon the prices at which shares are bought and sold on the exchange. But if there should be some apparently permanent fall in the value of any of the company's investments — below their initial acquisition costs — then some provision for that diminution in value should be made and shown in the balance sheet. To do otherwise would be to misrepresent the worth of these assets.

(No suggestion is made here of recording an increase in the value of a firm's investments in the shares, loan stock and debentures of other companies. It is considered to be financially prudent to take note of apparently permanent losses in value as soon as they are revealed. Where increases in value occur, these should be brought into the accounts as soon as the gains are realised in cash. On the other hand, increasing the book values of fixed assets has a totally different objective. It attempts to show the current cost of being in business: it does *not* reflect a saleable value of the fixed assets.)

Within the context of the balance sheet item describing the firm's investments in shares, loan stock and debentures, the term 'cost' means the balance of the purchase price of the investments after deducting therefrom the expenses of their acquisition; investment acquisition expenses such as brokerage and commission charges should be charged to the profit and loss account at the time of purchase.

Finally where a company such as the Growing Company owns more than 10 per cent of the equity capital of some other company (not being a subsidiary) then the former company must give details of those firms in which it has these specified interests. Such details must also be given where any investment in shares amounts to at least 10 per cent of the assets shown in the balance sheet of the holding company. The required information includes

1   The name of the company whose shares are held.
2   The place of incorporation or registration.
3   Specifications of the class of shares held.
4   Proportion which the numbers of shares held bears to number of shares of that class which have been issued.

Disclosures of the names of firms whose shares are listed amongst the assets of a company does not end here. Where a company is a holding or parent company, then it must reveal the names — and much other data — of its subsidiary companies. All this disclosure of information acts to give the financial analyst or intending investor a better appreciation of the worth of corporate assets. At least it will show if too great a proportion of a company's wealth is tied up in one trade product or firm.

Current assets

Current assets are not intended to be held permanently or for any lengthy period. They are continually on the move as a result of trading operations. When raw material stocks are issued to the shop floor they enter the production process and become work-in-progress. Work-in-progress is fashioned into saleable commodities which are shown in the balance sheet as finished goods. When these goods are sold on credit, they are delivered to a customer who is then listed amongst the current assets as a debtor. As soon as that debtor settles his account, cash flows to the company — the current asset 'cash' replacing the current asset 'debtor' — and the cycle of business operations is almost complete. It remains to decide what shall be done with the cash which has been paid by those who purchased the products sold by our company. Some of that money will be used to pay creditors who supply the company with the raw materials necessary for its business. Exhibit 4 shows why current assets are frequently called circulating assets. The exhibit portrays the continually changing content of the group of assets called 'current

Exhibit 4

CIRCULATING ASSETS

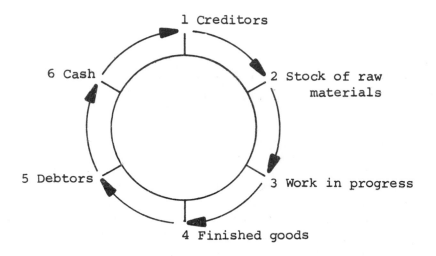

assets'. It shows the stages in the business of trading and the making of profit. The value of the individual product at each stage of its conversion from raw material to cash should be steadily increasing.

The Growing Company's current assets will be listed in its balance sheet as shown in Exhibit 5. They come after fixed assets and after investments in the ordering of assets on the right-hand side of the balance sheet.

The Companies Act, 1967, requires that the method of computing the value of stock-in-trade or. work-in-progress should be given IF those values are material for a proper appraisal of the company's state of affairs or of its profit or loss for the financial year. Now the process of valuing a stock of raw materials must commence with its actual cost of acquisition. But the determination of cost can be influenced by opinion because different values may be attributed to the same physical quantity of stock left in the storehouse. Such different values can arise as a direct result of the choice of the method of allocating, amongst the expenses of production, a cost for those goods used up in production*. Whichever of the several cost allocation

Exhibit 5

THE GROWING COMPANY LIMITED

Balance Sheet as at 31 December 19..

	£	£
Fixed Assets		*385,000*
Investments		*75,000*
Interest in Subsidiaries		*135,000*
CURRENT ASSETS		
Raw material stocks	165,000	
Work in progress	120,000	
Finished goods	85,000	
Debtors	200,000	
Bank	40,000	
Cash in hand	5,000	615,000

methods is used, the term cost can mean more than just the purchase price of the goods. It may well include such direct expenses which were necessary to place that stock in its present location where it is available for use by the company. Once the *cost* of the raw material stock (stock-in-trade) has been determined, then the value at which such stock is shown in the balance sheet should not exceed that cost figure. In certain situations it may be necessary to accord a lower value than cost, to stocks recorded in the balance sheet. This action would result from the need to recognise that a fall in value — below cost price — *had taken place* and the consequent need to ensure that such a fall in value was properly and prudently written off to the profit and loss account.

*See L.E. Rockley, *Non-accountant's guide to finance*, Chapter 5, Business Books (1972).

When values other than cost are given to stocks shown in a company's balance sheet, appropriate descriptions of these other values may include

1   At the lower of cost or net realisable value.
2   At the lowest of cost, net realisable value or replacement price.
3   At cost less a provision to reduce the value to net realisable value.

The term 'net realisable value' is self-explanatory. It means the net amount that could be obtained from selling the stock (in normal trading operations) either in its present state, or when embodied in some other product. Furthermore any expenses that were necessary to the processes of disposal of the stock would be deducted in arriving at the net realisable value.

Work-in-progress presents problems of valuation also and these values will be recorded in the profit and loss accounts and balance sheets of the company. Clearly some part of the valuation of work-in-progress must be the cost of the raw materials being incorporated in the goods which are in the process of manufacture. Again wages paid and payable to the workmen, who have fashioned the material up to its present state, should be regarded as part of the valuation. Now these concepts of value for the various kinds of stock, are really expressions of the total direct costs (the essential costs) which are being incurred because production is taking place. But the important thing is that the resultant commodity must be saleable. Should the business fail then it is very likely that the work-in-progress would have a scrap value only. After all the materials used would have been 'mutilated' in manufacture and unless some other company wants those precise pieces of unfinished work, there would be no market, other than the scrap market where the work-in-progress could be sold. The same circumstances will arise where there is a sudden marked change in consumer taste or fashions which acts to reduce or eliminate any demand for the firm's output. Therefore whilst it has been suggested that the relevant manufacturing wages should be brought into the valuation of work-in-progress, these valuations are merely reflecting an expectation of business continuance. They reflect, moreover, an expectation of sale of the eventually finished goods at a price greater than the valuations given.

However this is not all. One can say that goods in the process of manufacture are using the facilities of the whole firm. Machines are available for the workmen to operate, special tools are used, expenditure is incurred on progressing and planning the production, inspection of the work may take place at various stages in the manufacturing process — all these items represent some of the *capacity* costs of being able to manufacture the goods in question.

In fact any expense short of the selling and distribution costs will be contributing to the output of the works. The problem is, should some proportion of these overhead expenses be brought into the work-in-progress valuation?

But many of the so called overhead expenses do not vary in relation to the level of output. On the contrary they are determined by the passage of time (once the decision is taken to establish the firm in the first place). Such overhead expenses are better described by the term 'period expenses' because they relate to a specific period and NOT primarily to a certain level of production. Examples of period expenses will include depreciation, salaries, supervisory wages, rent, rates, insurance and so on. Nevertheless the reader will encounter well reasoned instances where period overhead expenses are included for work-in-progress valuations.

A final comment on stock valuation will concern finished goods. These should be valued at cost (see above) but care should be taken to ensure that the finished goods are in a saleable condition in relation to the values at which they are shown in the balance sheet.

The remaining principal current asset, apart from cash in hand and bank deposits, relates to the firm's debtors. They represent the money owing to the company in consequence of its credit sales. The values recorded should show the amount of cash which the company expects to receive from those who have purchased its goods on credit. Where the settlement of any of these debts appears to be in doubt, or where some reduction in the amounts, due e.g. to discount, is expected then the value of those debtors should be reduced accordingly in the balance sheet.

The balance sheet of the Growing Company has been devised to include the most frequently encountered type of current asset. The list which has been examined above is not an exhaustive one. For example the reader may know of certain companies where some investments are shown amongst the current assets. This could hapoen where a temporary cash surplus was being put to some profitable use rather than being left in a non-interest bearing current account. Such investments would not be held for trading influences or business control purposes. As soon as the need for cash re-asserted itself, the short-term kind of investment would be sold: truly an asset of the current period only. Again such items as Bills Receivable, Prepayments and Goods Out on Approval might be found in the current assets section of a balance sheet. But the object of this publication is not to deal at length with all possible combinations of balance sheet assets. The intention and need is to provide you, the reader, with a basic framework of knowledge which we can use subsequently in the analysis of corporate final accounts.

Exhibit 6

THE GROWING COMPANY LIMITED

Balance Sheet as at 31 December 19..

	£
Fixed Assets	*385,000*
Investments	*75,000*
Interest in Subsidiaries	*135,000*
Current Assets	*615,000*
CAPITAL EXPENSES	
Expenses of issue of shares	40,000

Capital expenses

The items found in this section of a balance sheet are also known as Fictitious Assets or as Deferred Charges. In fact nothing saleable will be found in the Capital Expenses part of any balance sheet. Capital expenses may consist of the costs of starting up a company, or the costs of issuing shares or debentures. It would be unreasonable to charge the whole of such costs to any part of the profit and loss account relating to the year in which those expenses were incurred. Expenses of this nature do not relate to one year's trading only. They are part of the costs of establishing a continuing business and logically they could be spread over all the profit and loss accounts which will be prepared during the firm's expected life. In practice however it is customary to write them off against trading income within a period of two or three years only. To the extent that amounts for such items are shown in any balance sheet, the actual charging of these sums to a profit and loss account has been *deferred* to some later account(s) - hence the term *deferred charges*. (The sort of deferred expenditure - expenses for which a full charge to the profit and loss account has been deferred to later year(s) - which may be found in this section of a balance sheet will include

1   The preliminary expenses of starting up a company.
2   Any expenses relating to the issue of any shares or debentures.
3   Any commissions paid in respect of the issue of shares or debentures.

4   Any amounts allowed by way of discount in respect of any
    shares or debentures.
[*The Companies Act, 1967*, Schedule 2, paragraph 3])
    The relevant balance sheet entries will appear as shown in Exhibit
6.

Sources of funds

We have now examined the balance sheet evidence of the disposal of
funds received by the company and we have some knowledge of the
company's possessions as they existed and were valued at the date of
that balance sheet.

    The picture will now be completed by a study of the various types
of financial resources — funds and credit — which enabled the firm to
acquire the assets already listed in the previous exhibits.

Authorised capital

The authorised capital of a company is nothing more than a statement of the number and classification of the shares which the firm
is *empowered* to issue. The detail of the various types of shares
which a firm can issue will also be found in its Memorandum of
Association. Now the Memorandum describes the company's powers
and its relationship with the outside world. It states amongst other
things
1   The company's name, ending with the word 'Limited'.
2   The objects of the company (which will take the form of a
    comprehensive list of the activities for which the company has
    been established and may wish to undertake).
3   The location of the registered office.
4   Details of the firm's share capital and that the liability of the
    members is limited.
The information is registered with the Registrar of Companies and
the company effecting such a registration will have to pay a duty
which is based upon the nominal value of the shares included in its
proposed authorised capital. Thus the authorised capital is sometimes called the 'Registered Capital'.

    Should the Growing Company Limited wish to increase its *issued*
share capital beyond its stated *authorised* capital, then it would first
have to secure an increase in the currently registered authorised
capital. The procedure for increasing authorised capital will be stated
in the company's own regulations and approval of such increases may

be relatively smoothly accomplished. Capital duty will have to be paid on face or nominal value of the increased number of shares in the revised authorised capital.

On the other hand the process of reducing the total value of the company's capital is a more serious matter and the principle of a reduction of share capital must be authorised by the Articles of Association of the company. The importance of the Articles of Association is emphasised here in that they govern the internal management of the company's business and will normally state explicitly the rights of the various classes of shareholder. A clear statement of shareholder's rights will be most valuable when reductions of capital are being considered: at least a statement, about the way in which total capital reduction is to be apportioned amongst the various classes of shareholder, would be expected.

Any specific proposal for reducing the capital of a company must

1   Be approved by a special resolution passed by the company's shareholders.

2   Be subject to confirmation by the Courts.

Moreover 'reducing the capital' of a company can refer to either the issued or the nominal value of the shares. In other words the nominal value of the shares may be reduced, and/or the actual paid-up value of the issued shares may be reduced.

Exhibit 7 shows how the authorised capital is detailed in a limited company's balance sheet. This section of the balance sheet is separately totalled. The figures which denote the amounts of the authorised capital are NOT included in the summation of the liabilities as shown on the left hand side of the balance sheet. This is because they do not represent money owed or funds received by the company: the authorised capital is a statement of share issuing *power* only.

Issued capital

Whilst the authorised capital shows the total amount and classification of the shares which a company may issue, the issued capital section of a balance sheet (see Exhibit 8) shows what has actually been issued.

It should be noted that each individual share, in both the authorised and the issued capital is described by giving it a financial value. Thus we find that the Growing Company's share capital includes '250,000 Ordinary shares of £1 each'. That financial value, £1, is termed the face value or nominal value. It does not necessarily indicate the price at which the shares were sold to the shareholder. It is merely 'the division (of capital) into shares of a fixed amount' and serves to identify that share as a fixed proportion of the whole capital of the

Exhibit 7
THE GROWING COMPANY LIMITED
Balance Sheet as at 31 December 19..

	£		£
AUTHORISED CAPITAL		*Fixed Assets*	*385,000*
100,000 6% Preference shares		*Investments*	*75,000*
of £1 each	100,000	*Interest in Subsidiaries*	*135,000*
300,000 Ordinary shares of £1 each	300,000	*Current Assets*	*615,000*
		Capital Expenses	*40,000*
	£400,000		

Exhibit 8
THE GROWING COMPANY LIMITED
Balance Sheet as at 31 December 19..

	£		£		£
Authorised Capital			400,000	*Fixed Assets*	*385,000*
ISSUED CAPITAL				*Investments*	*75,000*
50,000 6% Preference				*Interest in Subsidiaries*	*135,000*
shares of £1 each	50,000			*Current Assets*	*615,000*
250,000 Ordinary shares				*Capital Expenses*	*40,000*
of £1 each	250,000		300,000		

company. Each Ordinary share thereby carries an entitlement to that proportion of the corporate profit which remains after all other prior capital (such as Preference shares) has been paid its reward. Moreover the dividend percentage which a company declares on its Ordinary shares is based upon that nominal value. In this matter it is important to realise that the declared dividend is NOT stated as a percentage of the market price of the share — a 10 per cent dividend payable to the Ordinary shareholders of the Growing Company would mean a dividend of 10p, i.e. 10 per cent of £1.

In the event of the company winding up or where other circumstances result in the return of corporate wealth to the shareholders the nominal value of an Ordinary share, being a fixed proportion of the total issued Ordinary share capital, determines the share of the net corporate wealth which is available for such a shareholder.

Preference shares

Companies may specify more than one type of share in their authorised and issued capitals. In addition to the Ordinary shares referred to above, there are various types of Preference share. Now a Preference shareholder is entitled to his dividend in priority to the Ordinary shareholder*. The amount of an annual preference dividend is shown in the description of the Growing Company's share capital, 6 per cent. Thus the company's issued capital includes '50,000 6 per cent Preference shares'. In addition to the expectation of an annual dividend of a stated amount, the Preference shareholder may enjoy further preferential treatment with regard to the return of his capital sum. If the company should cease its operations, the Preference shareholder will most likely be assured of receiving the nominal value of his shareholding returned to him, before the Ordinary shareholder is paid anything. It should be remembered, of course, that these events will depend upon sufficient cash being realised from the sale of the firm's assets, to pay shareholders anything at all.

The reader should note that there are several types of Preference share. The descriptions accorded to these various types are

*All of the comments about dividends payable to the various classes of shareholder assume that the directors of the company do recommend that a dividend be paid. This is the prerogative of the directors, NOT of the shareholders. The articles will normally be explicit on this point and will most likely state that no dividend shall be payable in excess of that recommended by the directors. At the annual general meeting the shareholders can ratify the proposed dividend or they can suggest a lower rate. They cannot normally approve a higher rate of dividend than that proposed.

1   Cumulative Preference shares.
2   Participating Preference shares.
3   Cumulative Participating Preference shares.
4   Redeemable Preference shares.

The first category refers to Preference shares that carry an entitlement to receive their full dividend, up to date, before any Ordinary shareholder is paid. Thus if there is insufficient profit in any year to pay that year's preference dividend, then the unpaid dividend amount would be a first claim on the *distributable* profits of subsequent years. The Ordinary shareholders would not receive any dividend payment until the past and present Preference dividend entitlement was fully met.

Participating Preference shares have a right to a fixed annual dividend though this is not a cumulative right, i.e. one which accumulates year by year in the event of non-payment, as it is for the cumulative Preference shares. In some compensation for the non-cumulative aspect of these shares the participating Preference shareholder takes part in a further distribution of profit, in addition to his fixed annual rate, *after* the Ordinary shareholders have been paid a specified minimum rate of dividend. However the cumulative participating Preference shares combine the best features of both of the above mentioned special types of share.

Redeemable Preference shares

Redeemable Preference shares are the only type of share where the holder is entitled to repayment of his capital from the company, without having to wait for the company to close down. The second schedule to *The Companies Act, 1967,* states that a company's balance sheet must specify:

> 'any part of the issued capital that consists of redeemable preference shares, the earliest and latest dates on which the company has power to redeem those shares, whether those shares must be redeemed in any event, or are liable to be redeemed at the option of the company and whether any (and if so, what,) premium is payable on redemption'

For example, if the Growing Company's Preference shares were redeemable and this repayment was contracted to take place between 1 January 1983 and 31 December 1988 ('the earliest and latest dates'), then the balance entry for the shares would be

       50,000 6% Redeemable Preference shares
          (1983/1988) of £1 each   50,000

Now one of the features of a limited liability company is that its shareholders (except the above-mentioned redeemable Preference shareholders) do not have their capital returned to them whilst the firm is still in existence. The proprietors of a limited liability company should not receive any special treatment such as would put the interests of the company's creditors and other lenders, in jeopardy. Consequently the presence of redeemable Preference shares in the capital structure of a company demands that certain safeguards are established with the object of preserving the total amount of the company's issued capital and reserves and to protect the interests of all other creditors of the firm. The safeguards are specified in *The Companies Act, 1948*, section 58 and they require that

1   An issue of redeemable Preference shares must be authorised by the firm's Articles of Association.
2   Redeemable Preference shares can be redeemed only where they are fully paid up (see below).
3   When such shares are redeemed, the total sum (apart from any premium payable on redemption) due to the shareholders must be provided out of profits available for dividends OR out of the proceeds of a new issue of shares which were issued specifically to provide for the redemption.

Any premium which may be payable when the shares are redeemed *must* be met either out of profits or it must be charged to a share premium account (see page 23). As if this was not enough, a final requirement lays down that when Preference shares are redeemed out of profits, a special reserve must be created. The special reserve must be equal in amount to the total nominal value of the shares redeemed. Such a special reserve cannot be distributed in the form of dividends to shareholders, though it may be used to issue bonus shares. Thus

1   Profits are retained in the business.
2   The total amount of the company's issued capital and permanent reserves is maintained.
3   Cash resources are not dissipated because profits are kept in the business.
4   The interests of other creditors are safeguarded.

Amounts paid to the company for its shares

So far we have considered the share capital of the Growing Company as though all the monies due on issue of the shares have been paid by the shareholder to the company. For this reason the Growing Company's shares could be styled 'fully paid up'. But in some instances shareholders pay for their shares by instalments, an availability which would be detailed in the prospectus relating to the particular share issue. If for example only 50p of the Ordinary shares' nominal value had been demanded they would be described as '50p paid' and would appear in the balance sheet as follows

```
                                                          £

     250,000 Ordinary shares of £1 each
         (50p paid)                                   125,000
```

The point to note here is that a dividend of 10 per cent would amount to 5p per share — 10 per cent of 50p NOT 10 per cent of the full nominal value.

A final comment on the subject of issued share capital concerns shares that are issued at a price higher than their nominal value. Clearly the worth of a share depends upon the earning power of the assets which stand behind the share. An expectation by investors of high future earnings by a company will result in a higher rather than a lower share price being quoted on the stock market. In these circumstances if a company decided to issue an additional quantity of Ordinary shares, they could be issued at a price greater than their nominal or face value. The amount by which the issue price of a share exceeds its nominal value is called the share premium. The total amount of the premiums on all such shares must be carried to a special reserve which is recorded in the balance sheet and is called the 'share premium account'. This is a reserve of particular interest; it cannot be used to pay dividends and it is a part of the permanent (reserve) capital of the company. It will be discussed further in the next section of this balance sheet study.

Reserves

When a company begins its activities, its balance sheet will not normally be a complicated one. The statement of its owings and ownings could appear as shown in Exhibit 9. The example is a very simple one. The source of funds, 20,000 Ordinary shares is revealed as the whole of the company's liabilities. It owes nothing to any other person or group of persons. If we now assume that the entire stock of trading goods was sold on credit for £6,000, a new balance sheet if it was presented as in Exhibit 10 would show that the asset

Exhibit 9

NEW COMPANY LIMITED

Balance Sheet as at ....

	£		£
Issued Capital		*Fixed Assets*	15,000
20,000 Ordinary shares of £1 each	20,000	*Current Assets*	
		Stocks	5,000
	£20,000		£20,000

Exhibit 10

NEW COMPANY LIMITED

Balance Sheet as at ....

	£		£
Issued Capital		*Fixed Assets*	15,000
20,000 Ordinary shares of £1 each	20,000	*Current Assets*	
		Debtors	6,000
	£20,000		£21,000

value of the company was greater than the funds originally supplied to it.

To correct the imbalance shown in the above statement, the left-hand side of the balance sheet needs to be increased by £1,000 — the profit earned in the trading venture. Therefore the sum of £1,000 must be listed amongst the company's reserves and the firm would be shown as owing £21,000, which would agree with the book value of its possessions. The new total of the corporate liabilities will be comprised of

£20,000 which was subscribed by shareholders when the shares were first issued

PLUS

£1,000 profit which was gained through trading activities.

Exhibit 11 shows the new balance sheet with this data recorded therein. The balance sheet emphasises the nature of a reserve: it is a measure of growth in wealth of the company. It is NOT an indicator of cash assets possessed by the company. Exhibits 5 and 12 will confirm this fact. Exhibit 5 shows that the Growing Company has cash and bank resources of £45,000 whilst the firm's reserves total £475,000 as detailed in Exhibit 12.

Each of these reserves has arisen in consequence of some growth in the company's net wealth. A growth in net wealth describes an increase in the monetary value of the proprietors' investment in the business, over and above the face value of the shares they possess. That increase in wealth belongs to the proprietors and is therefore shown, in any balance sheet, immediately adjacent to the section called issued capital. When the separate amounts of Issued Capital and Reserves are totalled they aggregate to what is called, and is noted in a balance sheet as, 'Total Shareholders' Interest'.

The Growing Company's reserves include a Share Premium of £148,000. This is an account which has been discussed on page 23. It derives from the additional sums or values received by the firm, in excess of the nominal value of the shares which have been issued. The presence of a share premium account evidences the fact that the company has been able to issue shares at a higher price than the purely nominal value inscribed on each share certificate. The share premium account is a statutory reserve; it cannot be used to issue dividends, though it may be used to issue bonus shares to existing shareholders.

The Revaluation Reserve on the other hand does not represent any part of the firm's source of cash. It reflects a specific growth in wealth which has arisen as a result of the possession of physical

Exhibit 11
NEW COMPANY LIMITED
Balance Sheet as at ......

	£		£
Issued Capital		Fixed Assets	15,000
20,000 Ordinary shares of £1 each	20,000	Current Assets	
Reserves		Debtors	6,000
Profit and loss account	1,000		
	£21,000		£21,000

Exhibit 12
THE GROWING COMPANY LIMITED
Balance Sheet as at 31 December 19..

	£	£		£
Authorised Capital		400,000	Fixed Assets	385,000
Issued Capital		300,000	Investments	75,000
RESERVES			Interest in Subsidiaries	135,000
Share premium	148,000		Current Assets	615,000
Revaluation reserve	100,000		Capital Expenses	40,000
General reserve	192,000			
Profit and loss account				
balance	35,000			
		475,000		

assets. These assets, and we refer here to fixed assets, have increased to a value in excess of that shown in previous balance sheets. Generally, the influences of inflation will have brought about changes such as these. But if a more realistic view is to be taken of the asset worth of the company, then it is a sound practice to show these increases in value in the balance sheet. At the same time the growth in corporate asset wealth must be matched by a similar growth in the Total Shareholders' Interest. The result is the creation of a Revaluation Reserve.

Finally the reader is referred to the General Reserve and the Profit and Loss Account balance. These are reserves of a similar nature for they arise from the same source — profitable trading. When a firm makes a profit then the worth of the corporate net assets will increase. To the extent that this increase in worth is retained in the business (some of the increase in wealth is paid to shareholders in the form of dividend and some is paid to the Government in taxation) it will be represented by the balance on the Profit and Loss account plus the balance on the General Reserve. This is because the General Reserve is formed out of the post-tax profits earned by the company. The same arithmetical result would be achieved, in the Growing Company's balance sheet, if the Profit and Loss account had been shown as £227,000 and no General Reserve had been created.

But the existence of a General Reserve carries with it certain implications concerning the use to which corporate profits may have been devoted. The reader must remember that profits earned represent increases in a company's net wealth. When these profits are retained in the company — sometimes called 'ploughing back' the earnings — they may well be located amongst the increases in the firm's fixed and current assets. Such asset increases portray extensions of business activity which the firm has paid for out of its own profitable operations (that is, those asset increases which are financed from profits as distinct from those financed from borrowing or new share business). The business is growing in physical asset size and that growth will come to be regarded as a *permanent* development of the company.

For these reasons, the directors may decide that a certain proportion of the profits should be retained in the business and not paid away in, for example, dividends. A General Reserve would be an indication of this fact: it demonstrates the amount of past profits which are (a) deemed to be invested in the business' essential assets and (b) are not expected therefore to be used for dividends. The General Reserve *could* be used for shareholders' dividends, but it may be very desirable that it should not be so used.

Exhibit 13

THE GROWING COMPANY LIMITED

Balance Sheet as at 31 December 19..

	£		£
Authorised Capital	400,000	Fixed Assets	385,000
Issued Capital	300,000	Investments	75,000
		Interest in Subsidiaries	135,000
Reserves	475,000	Current Assets	615,000
LONG-TERM LOANS		Capital Expenses	40,000
6% Debentures	100,000		

Exhibit 13 presents another group of items found on the liabilities side of the balance sheet — Long-term Loans or as frequently described, Loan Capital. Long-term loans include debentures, loan stock and bank loans: these are terms which denote funds which are lent to a company for periods in excess of one year. More often we shall find that such loans are made for 5, 10 or 15 years and over.

Now the principal form of long-term loan is the debenture. A debenture is a document which evidences the fact that the owner thereof has lent money, to a business, for a specified period. An annual rate of interest is payable and is prescribed in the debenture deed. In some instances the capital sum is secured against certain of the company's assets. Thus the risk of loss for the lender is minimised. Should debenture holders' capital and interest appear to be in jeopardy then a trustee acting for the debenture holders may take possession of the mortgaged assets and so use or sell them to ensure payment of all sums due to the debenture holders.

Not all debentures have this safeguard: some are styled 'unsecured' or 'naked' debentures. Such loans do not carry the right to take and sell specified corporate assets in discharge of sums due by the company. On the other hand, secured debentures can inhibit the freedom of the company's managers. In such circumstances, corporate assets mortgaged to the debenture holders could not be sold by the firm without first securing permission from those lenders to whom the assets were mortgaged. As a result business reorganisations, involving replacement of assets wearing out, would have to be approved by the secured lenders before management could go ahead with its plans. To meet this problem the *floating* charge debenture has been developed. Here the lender's security is not provided by a mortgage against particular assets but by a charge which is spread over — floats over — certain types of assets. In this way the company is free to deal with the individual physical items of plant and machinery, etc., in the normal course of business. But should the company default on any of the payments due to the lender, the floating charge is said to crystallise. It then becomes a charge upon any of the separate assets falling within that class of asset against which the floating charge was secured.

A company's power to issue debentures will be limited principally in two ways. These constraints refer to a business' need to have

1   A sufficiency of long-life assets available to pledge as security for the capital money lent.
2   A sufficiency of regular income to cover the annual interest payments due to the lender.

Corporate liquidity is of vital importance when the company's financial structure includes an issue of debentures. The debenture holders' annual interest and his capital sum must be secure. Certainly the annual interest must be paid in each year whether the firm is profitable or not. To limit a business' financing risks therefore, debenture issue documents will normally contain terms and conditions for redemption of the stock. They may state the price at which repayment should take place and/or the period during which such repayments may be effected. Debenture stock redemption does not envisage necessarily, private transactions with individual stockholders only: it can involve purchases by the company on the open market, even before the expiry of the loan period. Thus the management may decide to use some of the earnings gained in years of good profits to repay (all or) a proportion of the debenture holders.

Again debenture holders may have the right to convert their holdings into Ordinary shares. The rate at which debentures could be exchanged for Ordinary shares would be specified in the prospectus relevant to the debenture issue. Two advantages accrue to a business when debenture holders opt to convert their stock into Ordinary shares: these advantages are

1   The cancellation of debenture stocks upon their conversion to Ordinary shares leads to a reduction in the company's financing risks, and in the potential constraints upon its management.
2   The avoidance of a sudden reduction in the corporate liquidity — a situation which would arise when debenture holders are repaid their capital sum.

Loan stock may be issued direct to the public, and therefore can result in a large issue being subscribed by many individual lenders: a convenient way of obtaining funds from numerous sources. Loan stock can be issued direct to specific financing groups such as the insurance companies. Alternately a debenture rights issue may be offered to company shareholders. Such an issue enables the firm's proprietors to lend money to the firm, through the purchase of debenture stock, and it keeps the interest of the business 'in the family'.

Clearly, issues of loan stock cannot be recommended for all types of company. Where a firm's business is of a predominantly risky nature, profits can vary quite substantially. Here the ability to pay annual debenture interest may be in some doubt. Therefore for a speculative operation, or where returns are subject to wide fluctuation, financing by loan stock should not be considered. Indeed it is most likely that an issue of loan stock would not succeed on the market. The reader must remember that a purchaser of loan stock (the debenture holder) looks for the security of his annual interest and the eventual return of his capital sum.

Yet loan stock issues can be of considerable benefit to firms which are not constrained by fluctuating profits or by the lack of mortgagable assets. Such an issue can provide — for the right firms — a sound base of funds at a rate of interest which is fixed for the term of the loan. Better long range planning of the firm's activities can be undertaken. Nevertheless loan stock issues are not normally recommended for the early years of a firm's life. The lack of an adequate record to indicate the firm's expected ability to meet annual interest charges, is the reason. Furthermore the amount of annual interest charges might be a too embarrassing burden for a developing business to accept.

Current liabilities

Our study of the Growing Company's balance sheet ends with an examination of the Current Liabilities (see Exhibit 14). These have been described as the company's liabilities of the current period. In most instances they comprise debts owed by the firm and which must be settled within a relatively short period. The majority of the current liabilities will be discharged by the Growing Company within a month or two: all should be discharged within 12 months at the most.

The item 'Trade creditors' relates to amounts owing by the company for supplies of raw materials, components or other goods which the business uses in its trading activities. These goods which are purchased for consumption in the firm's manufacturing and trading operations will be received into the firm's stores and eventually issued to the shop floor. To the extent that raw material supplies remain unused in the storehouse at the date of the balance sheet, such unused stocks will appear in the balance sheet amongst the current assets at an appropriate value (see Exhibit 5 on page 13).

It is likely that much of the material supplied on credit will be passed into the production process before the creditor is paid. This does not mean that the purchaser is always able to sell his final product before paying the amounts due to the raw material supplier. The length of the production process, the time lag before a finished good becomes a sale, and the period of credit taken by the purchasers of the finished goods before they pay for their purchases — all these events conspire to ensure that suppliers of raw materials will have to be paid before the business obtains a cash flow from its own sales. For reasons such as these a business needs working capital.

Creditors for raw materials and other goods from the major part,

Exhibit 14

THE GROWING COMPANY LIMITED

Balance Sheet as at 31 December 19..

	£	£		£
Authorised Capital		400,000	*Fixed Assets*	385,000
			Investments	75,000
Issued Capital		300,000	*Interest in Subsidiaries*	135,000
Reserves		475,000	*Current Assets*	615,000
Long-term Loans		100,000	*Capital Expenses*	40,000
CURRENT LIABILITIES				
Trade creditors	215,000			
Expenses due	35,000			
Current taxation	20,000			
Future taxation	35,000			
Bills payable	70,000			
Overdraft at bank	—			
		375,000		

in value, of most firm's current liabilities. Other unpaid expenses include amounts due, at the date of the balance sheet, for wages, rent, rates, insurance and similar services. These items appear in the balance sheet as debts due to be paid by the business, not because the firm is deliberately slow in settling its debts. They arise because wages are paid in arrear and because bills and invoices for other services are received long after the particular service has been consumed in the manufacturing and trading process. These costs will have been listed amongst the expenditures in the profit and loss account, but because certain specific amounts remain unpaid at the date of the balance sheet, they must be shown as current liabilities in the balance sheet.

Taxation

The current liabilities also contain two items of taxation. This practice of showing two taxation liabilities amongst the current debts conform with that found in many published accounts. The presence of the two separate debts arises because the profits of a company in accounting year 1 are used as a basis for calculating that company's taxation payment in accounting year 2. Furthermore the assessed amount due for accounting year 2 will be payable on 1 January next following the end of that financial year. There is therefore a time lag before the business has to pay the tax due on any year's profits. In the Growing Company's balance sheet the amount which is payable on 1 January next is called 'Current taxation'. This debt has not been based upon the current profits, i.e. those appearing in the profit and loss account which will accompany the particular balance sheet we are studying. The assessment of £20,000 for taxation *currently* due would be derived from those profits shown in the previous year's profit and loss account.

So far as the current year's profits are concerned the estimate of the tax which is presently expected to be assessed on those profits has been set at £35,000. This is a liability for tax in the future and is therefore called 'Future taxation'. After the estimated amount has been appropriately revised, the revised sum due — the finally assessed taxation debt will become the 'current taxation' entry in next year's balance sheet. That amount will then become payable on 1 January following the date of next year's balance sheet. Therefore the heading Current Liabilities, under which these debts are shown, does not always describe the company's debts of the current period. It would seem therefore that the future taxation liability ought not to be shown amongst the current liabilities. It would be better located in

Exhibit 15

SOURCES OF COMPANY FUNDS

COMPANY

FROM INVESTMENT

1 The Industrial and Commercial Finance Corporation,
   and Finance Corporation for Industry are organi-
   sations coming between the banks and the stock
   market.* They meet the needs of the borrower of
   £5,000 and upwards.
2 In these cases, an interest in the equity is
   taken and the capital gearing is one of the
   important factors in negotiations leading to the
   loan.
3 Furthermore, the company, its directors, its managerial succession and its whole organisation will
   come under very close examination.

COMPANY

1 Ploughing back profits so as to develop earning
   capacity and stimulate profits.
2 Considerations of return on capital retained will
   be matched with good dividend status.
3 Expansion or new developments and diversification
   are considered with long-term stability

PUBLIC

SHARES

PREFERENCE
(a) Cumulative
(b) Non-cumulative
(c) Participating
(d) Redeemable

ORDINARY
(a) Deferred
(b) Preferred

(a) If the profit is insufficient
    in any year to pay the fixed
    dividend on these shares then
    such dividend arrears will be
    carried forward against future
    profits.
(b) Dividend arrears cannot be
    carried forward.
(c) Such shares are entitled to a
    fixed dividend in priority to Ordinary shares AND in
    addition they are entitled to a further share of any
    profit left after Ordinaries have had an agreed sum.
(d) Are repayable out of the proceeds of a new issue or
    from profits otherwise available for dividend.

(a) Frequently refer-
    red to as founders'
    shares and ranking
    after (b) as
    regards dividend
(b) They may have
    powerful voting
    rights

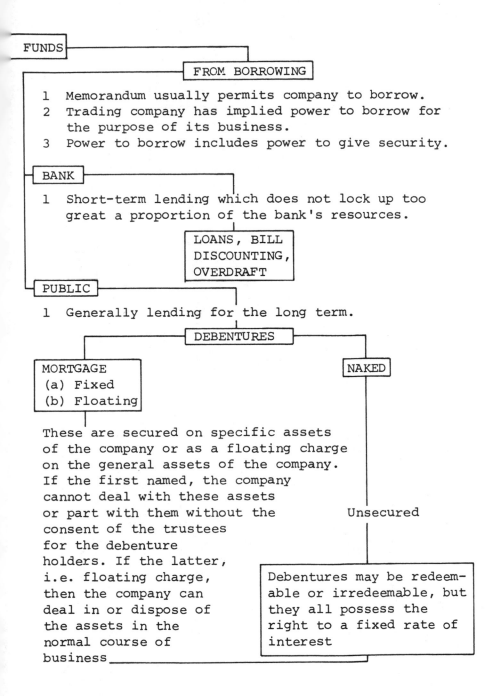

FUNDS

FROM BORROWING

1 Memorandum usually permits company to borrow.
2 Trading company has implied power to borrow for
  the purpose of its business.
3 Power to borrow includes power to give security.

BANK

1 Short-term lending which does not lock up too
  great a proportion of the bank's resources.

LOANS, BILL
DISCOUNTING,
OVERDRAFT

PUBLIC

1 Generally lending for the long term.

DEBENTURES

MORTGAGE
(a) Fixed
(b) Floating

NAKED

These are secured on specific assets
of the company or as a floating charge
on the general assets of the company.
If the first named, the company
cannot deal with these assets
or part with them without the
consent of the trustees
for the debenture
holders. If the latter,
i.e. floating charge,
then the company can
deal in or dispose of
the assets in the
normal course of
business

Unsecured

Debentures may be redeem-
able or irredeemable, but
they all possess the
right to a fixed rate of
interest

*Now merged into Finance for Industry.

Exhibit 16

THE GROWING COMPANY LIMITED

Balance Sheet as at 31 December 19..

Previous year £		£	£
	Authorised Capital		
100,000	100,000 6% Preference shares of £1 each	100,000	
300,000	300,000 Ordinary shares of £1 each	300,000	
£400,000			£400,000
	Issued Capital		
100,000	50,000 6% Preference shares of £1 each	50,000	
60,000	250,000 Ordinary shares of £1 each	300,000	

Previous year £		Cost or valuation £	Aggregate depreciation £	£
	Fixed Assets			
125,000	Land and buildings	250,000	75,000	175,000
120,000	Plant	358,000	198,000	160,000
45,000	Vehicles	60,000	20,000	40,000
10,000	Equipment	16,000	6,000	10,000
300,000		684,000	299,000	385,000
	Investments			
50,000	Quoted (MV £64,000)		50,000	
18,000	Unquoted (Directors' valuation £28,000)		25,000	
68,000				75,000

		Prior		
Reserves				
—	Share premium		148,000	
—	Revaluation reserve		100,000	
175,000	General reserve		192,000	
15,000	PL account bal.		35,000	
			475,000	
350,000	TOTAL SHAREHOLDERS' INTEREST			775,000
	Long-term Loans			
50,000	6% Debentures			100,000
	Current Liabilities			
150,000	Trade creditors	215,000		
40,000	Expenses	35,000		
20,000	Current taxation	20,000		
15,000	Future taxation	35,000		
25,000	Bills payable	70,000		
75,000	Overdraft at bank	—		
		375,000		
325,000				375,000
£725,000				£1,250,000

Interest in Subsidiaries				
—	Shares		125,000	
—	Amounts owing by subsidiary		25,000	
			150,000	
—	Amounts owing to subsidiary		15,000	
				135,000
Current Assets				
105,000	Raw material stocks	165,000		
94,000	Work in progress	120,000		
53,000	Finished goods	85,000		
101,000	Debtors	200,000		
—	Bank	40,000		
4,000	Cash in hand	5,000		
357,000				615,000
Capital Expenses				
—	Expenses on share issue			40,000
£725,000				£1,250,000

a group of items called 'Provisions' which would be placed immediately before the current liabilities section.

The remaining items, bills payable and bank overdraft, need little explanation. The former concerns bills of exchange which have been accepted by the company and will be redeemable within the current period. A bank overdraft is in effect a short-term loan which could be recalled, after a short period of notice has been given. For this reason it must be grouped amongst current liabilities and the fact, that successive balance sheets of a company may be showing a continuing bank overdraft, albeit of varying amounts, does not render the overdraft anything other than a *short-term* loan.

Conclusions

The various segments of the Growing Company's corporate worth have now been scrutinised. Before bringing these data together in a completed balance sheet, the reader is invited to study Exhibit 15. This exhibit describes the sources of funds for financing business operations and which have been discussed in the foregoing pages.

The whole balance sheet of our company is presented in Exhibit 16. It contains information additional to that shown in the previous exhibits. The balance sheet now shows, in respect of the *previous* year, the values which were then given to each of the assets and liabilities. The column which is headed 'Previous year' shows the financial and asset state of the Growing Company at the end of that year. By comparing the owings and ownings of the company at these two separate dates, much information about the firm's progress and development can be deduced. The reader will be invited to pursue the appraisal of the Growing Company in the following chapters.

Further reading

M. Greener, *Between the lines of the balance sheet,* Pergamon Press, (1968).

R. Sidebotham, *Introduction to the theory and context of accounting,* Pergamon Press (Second edition, 1970).

L.E. Rockley, *Finance for the non-accountant,* Business Books (1976). (See especially Chapters 1 - 3.)

R.A. Foulke, *Practical financial statement analysis,* McGraw-Hill (Fifth edition, 1961). (See especially Chapters I - IV.)

D. Goch, *Finance and accounts for managers,* Pan Books (Second Edition).

R.J. Chambers, 'The role of accounting', *The Accountant* (22 February 1969).

'Depreciation: its meaning, purpose and accounting treatment', *Accountancy,* pp. 73 - 84 (February 1969).

2 | *Balance Sheet Structure and Analysis*

The narrative balance sheet

In Chapter 1 our company's balance sheet was shown in conventional two-sided form with assets on the right hand side and liabilities on the left. Now there is no legal requirement for balance sheets to be presented in any particular way, though the data to be shown therein are closely specified by the Companies Acts. The published accounts of most limited companies display their balance sheet data in what is termed the 'narrative' or 'vertical' from. As an example of the narrative format, Exhibit 17 demonstrates how the Growing Company's balance sheet in Exhibit 16 can be redrawn in this alternative style.

The narrative method has many advantages, for it

1   Presents a more realistic combination of balance sheet items which —
2   Enables working capital and capital employed amounts to be clearly established and

Exhibit 17

THE GROWING COMPANY LIMITED

Balance Sheet as at 31 December 19..

Previous year £		Cost or valuation £	Aggregate depreciation £	£
	Fixed Assets			
125,000	Land and buildings	250,000	75,000	175,000
120,000	Plant	358,000	198,000	160,000
45,000	Vehicles	60,000	20,000	40,000
10,000	Equipment	16,000	6,000	10,000
300,000	TOTAL FIXED ASSETS	684,000	299,000	385,000
	Current Assets			
105,000	Raw material stocks		165,000	
94,000	Work in progress		120,000	
53,000	Finished goods		85,000	
101,000	Debtors		200,000	
–	Bank		40,000	
4,000	Cash in hand		5,000	
357,000			615,000	

Continued overleaf

	Col 1		Col 2	
Current Liabilities				
Trade creditors	150,000		215,000	
Expenses	40,000		35,000	
Current taxation	20,000		20,000	
Future taxation	15,000		35,000	
Bills payable	25,000		70,000	
Overdraft at bank	75,000		—	
	325,000		375,000	
WORKING CAPITAL	32,000			240,000
CAPITAL EMPLOYED	332,000			625,000
Investments				
Quoted (MV £64,000)	50,000		50,000	
Unquoted (DV £28,000)	18,000		25,000	
	68,000			75,000
Interest in Subsidiaries				
Shares	—		125,000	
Amounts owing by subsidiary	—		25,000	
			150,000	
Amounts owing to subsidiary	—		15,000	
				135,000
EMPLOYMENT OF LONG-TERM FUNDS	£400,000			£835,000

FUNDS EMPLOYED

	Issued Capital			
100,000	50,000 6% Preference shares of £1 each	50,000		
60,000	250,000 Ordinary shares of £1 each	250,000		300,000
	Reserves			
—	Share premium	148,000		
—	Revaluation reserve	100,000		
175,000	General reserve	192,000		
15,000	Profit and loss account balance	35,000		475,000
				775,000
—	*Less* Capital expenses not written off			40,000
350,000	NET WORTH OR TOTAL SHAREHOLDERS' INTEREST			735,000
	Long-term Loans			
50,000	6% Debentures			100,000
£400,000	TOTAL LONG-TERM FUNDS EMPLOYED			£835,000

3   Leads to a matching of the long-term funds invested in the company, with the book values of the net assets acquired thereby.

Moreover when a balance sheet and its corresponding profit and loss account are presented in narrative fashion, it becomes possible to display these two statements side by side. Relevant comparisons are more readily apparent and thus more easily made.

On occasions one can find a balance sheet which displays the details of one side of a conventional balance sheet immediately **above** the details of the other side. This style produces merely a vertical listing of balance sheet items: it gives no information additional to that found in the conventional layout: neither are the data grouped or linked in a more informative way. In brief, we shall not regard such a presentation as a narrative one. On the other hand, many public companies employ narrative formats which are excellent examples of the verticle style. Two such examples are given in Exhibits 18 and 19 where balance sheets, published by Courtaulds Limited and Tesco Limited, have been reproduced. Here emphasis is given to the long-term funds employed in the businesses which are then compared with the employment of those funds in financing fixed assets and working capital.

Both of the companies in Exhibits 18 and 19 adopt a similar approach to the display of Capital Employed and Employment of Capital. The reader will observe that Courtauld's has a quantity of fixed assets — capital assets — whilst Tesco does not. The latter is principally a holding company and thus is not a trading unit in itself but it controls its trading subsidiaries through its subsidiary company shareholdings. On the other hand Courtaulds is a parent company which is not confined to managing a number of subsidiary companies through appropriate shareholdings. The *parent* company has relevant capital assets of its own and has the ability to trade itself, through its possession of those capital assets.

An important feature of the two companies is demonstrated by the prominence given to the values of their working capitals. Courtauld's specifies its working capital (net current assets) as £124,032,000, £89,027,000 and £67,327,000 for the years 1974, 1973 and 1972, respectively: the figures are given in the balance sheet format. The increased investment in working capital over these three years is most marked but it does not result entirely from the increased activity which the company has generated during this period. However it will be more appropriate for us to study this aspect of the company's affairs when we examine the accounts of the *group* on page 53. Even so the current ratios for each of the three years are worth noting: they are 2.49, 2.83 and 2.83 for 1974, 1973 and 1972,

Exhibit 18

COURTAULDS LIMITED

Balance Sheets as at 31 March

	1974 £000	1973 £000	1972 £000
Capital Employed			
Preference capital	3,479	3,479	3,479
Ordinary capital	67,598	67,568	67,460
Reserves	170,381	127,859	102,239
NET WORTH OR TOTAL SHAREHOLDERS' INTEREST	241,458	198,906	173,178
Loan capital (long-term loans)	137,586	144,038	141,443
Deferred taxation	13,376	13,376	13,376
	£392,420	£356,320	£327,997
Employment of Capital			
Land, buildings, plant and equipment	103,189	95,345	83,196
Investment in subsidiaries	158,530	165,831	172,160
Other investments	6,669	6,117	5,314
	268,388	267,293	260,670
Current Assets			
Stocks	46,621	41,404	40,935
Debtors	8,095	16,378	21,473
Deposits	148,225	78,530	39,674
Cash	4,158	1,358	2,017
	207,099	137,670	104,099
Current Liabilities			
Creditors	65,820	28,745	23,226
Taxation	7,891	4,503	542
Dividends	9,356	15,395	13,004
	83,067	48,643	36,772
NET CURRENT ASSETS (WORKING CAPITAL)	124,032	89,027	67,327
	£392,420	£356,320	£327,997

Exhibit 19

TESCO STORES (HOLDINGS) LIMITED

Balance Sheets as at 24 February

CAPITAL EMPLOYED
Share capital
Share premium account
Unappropriated profits

Total share capital and reserves

Deferred taxation

EMPLOYMENT OF CAPITAL
Investments
Subsidiary companies:
  Shareholdings at cost
  Add Net amount due from
    subsidiary companies

Current assets:
  Debtors
  Cash and short-term deposits

Deduct: Current liabilities
  Creditors and accrued expenses
  Bank overdraft
  Current taxation
  Dividends

Deduct: Corporation tax payable on 1 Jan

	1974		1973		1972	
	£000	£000	£000	£000	£000	£000
		15,536		13,809		13,809
		5,432		7,193		7,193
		34,330		28,198		18,818
		55,298		49,200		39,820
		153		110		–
		£55,451		£49,310		£39,820
		4,184		7		–
	4,390		4,390		4,390	
	43,111	47,501	34,760	39,150	40,211	44,601
	407		402		48	
	10,410	10,817	15,329	15,731	260	308
		62,502		54,888		44,909
	712		470		513	
	–		–		1,780	
	1,784		880		77	
	3,493	5,989	4,020	5,370	2,620	4,990
		56,513		49,518		39,919
		1,062		208		99
		£55,451		£49,310		£39,820

respectively, and present a relatively satisfactory degree of liquidity. These ratios show that for every £1 of current liabilities the parent company had available current assets of £2.49 in 1974, £2.83 in 1973 and £2.83 again in 1972. A slight hardening of the situation is apparent, but nothing to be excited about.

Tesco does not *specify* its working capital in the balance sheet; it has to be calculated. In this calculation we must bring to the account, amongst the current liabilities, the Corporation Tax payable on the ensuing 1 January. In this way we recognise its essential nature as a short-term debt. Net current assets will then be revealed as

	1974 £000	1973 £000	1972 £000
Current assets	10,817	15,731	308
Current liabilities (plus Corporation Tax)	7,051	5,578	5,089
	£3,766	£10,153	(£4,781)
Current ratios	1.5	2.8	0.06

The balance sheet shows that the working capital has fluctuated sharply during the three-year period. From a negative balance in 1972 the net current assets had increased by £14,934,000 at the end of February 1973 whilst the following year saw a reduction of £6,387,000 by February 1974. The item which had the greatest impact on these fluctuations in current liquidity was each year's 'cash and short-term deposits'. The series of balance sheets reveal that this asset accounted for £10,410,000, £15,329,000 and £260,000 of the current assets in the years 1974, 1973 and 1972. When we study the company's actual and expected expansions of their stores outlets, we can understand that a planned availability of cash resources must be a feature of their financial management in order to be able to meet the capital expenditures from internal funds. The holding company has no bank overdraft and no loan stock.

The consolidated (or group) balance sheet

The three balance sheets — of the hypothetical Growing Company, of Courtaulds and of Tesco — present the asset/liability state of those companies with their controlling interests in other firms being described by the entry 'Investment (or Interest) in Subsidiaries'. Thus

the balance sheets do not show what assets the subsidiaries own at
the date of the statement, nor do they show what they owed. Without this additional information it is very difficult to appraise the principal firms' asset strength, their credit worthiness or profit performance. For these and other reasons a company which has subsidiaries must, at the end of its financial year, present accounts which amalgamate the separate balance sheets and profit and loss accounts of the subsidiaries with those of the holding or parent company. Such statements must be laid before a general meeting of the company. These requirements are specified at section 150 of *The Companies Act, 1948*, where amalgamations of balance sheets and profit and loss accounts are termed 'group accounts'.

Common practice also describes these combined statements as 'consolidated accounts'. Section 150 allows for exceptions to the requirement to produce group or consolidated accounts: these exceptions are

1   Where a company is the wholly owned subsidiary of another company.
2   Where a company's directors have the opinion that
   a   it is impracticable to produce group accounts, or that no real value would be achieved thereby or that the production of group accounts would involve expense or delay which would be out of proportion to the value of such accounts to the members of the parent company;
   b   the result would be misleading OR harmful to the company's business or any of its subsidiaries;
   c   the activities of the various firms — parent and subsidiaries — are so different that they cannot reasonably be treated as a single undertaking.

Where group accounts are not published for any of the above reasons, then much other data relating to the subsidiaries' profits will have to be given.

In order to pursue our study of the three companies therefore, we should use their appropriate *consolidated* balance sheets. Those for Courtaulds and Tesco are shown in Exhibits 22 and 23: we now have to devise a consolidated balance sheet for the hypothetical Growing Company. To this end we will assume that the Growing Company had acquired a 100 per cent controlling interest in its subsidiary X Limited on 31 December of year 2: this controlling interest is represented by the £125,000 which is shown in the Growing Company's balance sheet in Exhibit 16, under 'Interest in Subsidiaries'. Furthermore we will assume that the balance sheet of X, on that date, was as shown in Exhibit 20.

Armed with this information we can proceed to construct a

Exhibit 20

X LIMITED

Balance Sheet as at 31 December 19..

	£	£
Capital Employed		
Shares		20,000
Reserves		70,000
Net worth		£90,000
Employment of Capital		
Fixed assets		75,000
Current assets:		
Debtor - Growing Company	15,000	
Other debtors	60,000	
	75,000	
Current liabilities:		
Creditor - Growing Company	25,000	
Other creditors	35,000	
	60,000	
Net current assets		15,000
Total capital employed		£90,000

consolidated balance sheet for the group. Clearly the Growing Company has purchased a subsidiary which has a net worth of £90,000 and has paid £125,000 for its investment. The excess of the purchase price over the book value of X represents the cost to the Growing Company of obtaining control of X. The cost of control is £35,000 (£125,000 minus £90,000) and it will be shown in the Growing Company's consolidated balance sheet. At the same time the amounts due to and from X, as shown in the parent company's balance sheet will be used to eliminate the *corresponding* debtors and creditors found in X's balance sheet. The remaining assets and liabilities of both companies will then be aggregated to produce the consolidated balance sheet shown in Exhibit 21.

Exhibit 21

GROWING COMPANY LIMITED AND SUBSIDIARY X

Consolidated Balance Sheet as at 31 December 19..

	Year 2 £	Year 1 £
Capital Employed		
Share capital of parent company	300,000	160,000
Reserves	475,000	190,000
	775,000	350,000
Less capital expenses not written off	40,000	–
NET WORTH (or TOTAL SHARE-HOLDERS' INTEREST)	735,000	350,000
Loan capital	100,000	50,000
TOTAL LONG-TERM FUNDS EMPLOYED	£835,000	£400,000
Employment of Capital		
Cost of control (goodwill on consolidation)	35,000	–
Land, buildings, plant, equipment and vehicles	460,000	300,000
Investments	75,000	68,000
TOTAL FIXED ASSETS, INVESTMENTS AND GOODWILL	570,000	368,000
Current Assets		
Stocks	370,000	252,000
Debtors	260,000	101,000
Bank and cash	45,000	4,000
	675,000	357,000
Current Liabilities		
Creditors and accrued expenses	285,000	190,000
Taxation	55,000	35,000
Bills payable	70,000	25,000
Bank overdraft	–	75,000
	410,000	325,000
NET CURRENT ASSETS	265,000	32,000
EMPLOYMENT OF LONG-TERM FUNDS	£835,000	£400,000

For each of this company's assets and liabilities, the balance sheets in Exhibits 16, 17 and 21 show the corresponding amounts at the end of the immediately preceding financial year. This information must be given in accordance with the provisions of the second schedule of *The Companies Act, 1967*. Thus we have data which will tell us how the company has changed during the past 12 months. If we had two years' published accounts then we would be able to appraise the variations in company fortunes over a three-year period. Now it is most probable that a balance sheet issued by a UK limited company would appear as shown in Exhibit 21, but a statement drawn up in this way would not, by itself, disclose all of the information which a company is required to give. Therefore much additional data are given by way of explanatory notes which are attached to, or are published with, the final accounts.

Information accompanying the final accounts

With regard to fixed assets, the company must reveal the aggregate amount of fixed assets acquired during the year and the aggregate amount of fixed assets disposed of or destroyed during the year. Moreover when such assets are revalued then the published accounts, which first quote the revaluations, must state the names of the persons who valued them OR the valuers' qualifications for doing this work AND the bases of valuation used by them. Information such as is referred to above would be given in the notes of explanation which would accompany the balance sheet. Students of published balance sheets will find reference to the explanatory notes being given by an identification number at the side of the balance sheet item. The reference number will then lead the reader to the similarly numbered explanatory note which appears in a subsequent page in the published accounts booklet.

To demonstrate this process, and to prepare for our study of the various companies, the consolidated balance sheets of Courtaulds and Tesco are now shown in Exhibits 22 and 23.

In the annual accounts booklets published by the Tesco Group for 1974 and 1973, a reference number is noted clearly at the side of the balance sheet sub-heading 'Fixed Assets'. In the 1974 booklet the number given is 10; in the 1973 accounts it is 8 and by tracing these references in the detailed numbered notes which accompany each set of accounts, we can obtain much more information about the Group's fixed asset structure, its additions and extensions together with a breakdown of the annual depreciation charge. Exhibit 24 shows the movements in the Group's fixed assets over a three-year

Exhibit 22

COURTAULDS LIMITED AND SUBSIDIARIES

Group Balance Sheets as at 31 March

	1974 £000	1973 £000	1972 £000
CAPITAL EMPLOYED			
Preference capital	3,479	3,479	3,479
Ordinary capital	67,598	67,568	67,460
Reserves	284,739	219,781	183,147
Relating to Courtaulds Ltd	355,816	290,828	254,086
Minority interests	31,446	29,902	25,975
Loan capital	268,984	254,382	219,150
Deferred taxation	32,427	31,117	28,568
	£688,673	£606,229	£527,779
EMPLOYMENT OF CAPITAL			
Land, buildings, plant and equipment	354,161	300,377	290,097
Investments	16,727	13,347	11,861
FIXED ASSETS	370,888	313,724	301,958
Current Assets			
Stocks	224,176	194,720	181,723
Debtors	168,379	142,887	133,382
Deposits	206,817	121,831	58,255
Cash	6,105	12,392	12,326
	605,477	471,830	385,686
Current Liabilities			
Creditors	192,811	120,085	102,015
Overdrafts	63,087	33,722	35,771
Taxation	22,438	10,123	9,075
Dividends	9,356	15,395	13,004
	287,692	179,325	159,865
NET CURRENT ASSETS (WORKING CAPITAL)	317,785	292,505	225,821
	£688,673	£606,229	£527,779

Exhibit 23

TESCO STORES (HOLDINGS) LIMITED

Consolidated Balance Sheet as at 23-24 February

CAPITAL EMPLOYED
Issued capital of parent company
Share premium
Capital reserve
Unappropriated profits

TOTAL SHARE CAPITAL AND RESERVES

Amount set aside for anticipated losses
Deferred taxation

EMPLOYMENT OF CAPITAL
Fixed Assets
  Freeholds
  Leaseholds
  Plant, vehicles, equipment

TOTAL FIXED ASSETS

Investments

Current Assets
  Stocks at lower of cost or market value
  Debtors
  Cash and short-term deposits

Deduct: Current Liabilities
  Creditors and accrued expenses
  Current taxation
  Dividends

Deduct: Debentures secured on certain
  properties of a subsidiary company

Deduct: Corporation Tax payable on 1 January

| | 1974 | | 1973 | | 1972 | |
	£000	£000	£000	£000	£000	£000
		15,536		13,809		13,809
		5,432		7,193		7,193
		3,314		3,741		3,316
		35,704		29,553		20,183
		59,986		54,296		44,501
		1,000		–		–
		7,345		3,512		3,813
		£68,331		£57,808		£48,314
(10)			(8)			
		27,154		24,680		22,464
		13,334		10,615		9,006
		26,841		22,787		22,455
		67,329		58,082		53,925
		4,187		10		3
	47,934		31,031		28,034	
	4,729		3,116		2,501	
	13,244		16,426		1,558	
		65,907		50,573		32,093
		137,423		108,665		86,021
	51,979		35,506		26,596	
	4,201		2,712		2,322	
	3,493		4,020		2,620	
		59,673		42,238		31,538
		77,750		66,427		54,483
		546		609		647
		77,204		65,818		53,836
		8,873		8,010		5,522
		£68,331		£57,808		£48,314

Exhibit 24

MOVEMENTS IN FIXED ASSETS

FREEHOLDS at commencement
  Additions

Deduct: Disposals

BALANCE at 23-24 February

LEASEHOLDS at commencement
  Additions

Deduct: Disposals

  Amortisation

BALANCE at 23-24 February

PLANT, MOTOR VEHICLES, FIXTURES, FITTINGS
  AND EQUIPMENT at commencement
  Additions

Deduct: Disposals

  Depreciation

BALANCE at 23-24 February

1974		1973		1972	
Cost	Amounts written off	Cost	Amounts written off	Cost	Amounts written off
£000	£000	£000	£000	£000	£000
24,680	–	22,464	–	21,266	–
2,681	–	2,581	–	2,331	–
27,361		25,045		23,597	
207		365		1,133	
£27,154		£24,680		£22,464	
12,552	1,937	10,641	1,635	9,280	1,362
3,147	5	2,035	–	1,540	–
15,699	1,942	12,676	1,635	10,820	1,362
140	91	124	49	179	41
15,559	1,851	12,552	1,586	10,641	1,321
–	374	–	351	–	314
£15,559	£2,225	£12,552	£1,937	£10,641	£1,635
43,519	20,732	39,784	17,329	34,054	14,207
9,132	64	4,711	–	6,963	–
52,651	20,796	44,495	17,329	41,017	14,207
1,247	913	976	736	1,233	966
51,404	19,883	43,519	16,593	39,784	13,241
–	4,680	–	4,139	–	4,088
£51,404	£24,563	£43,519	£20,732	£39,784	£17,329

period; the table has combined the information given in the two sets of accounts for 1974 and 1973.

The notes published with the accounts give several other details about these fixed assets, but the statement in the above exhibit does present a very full account of the changes in the Group's fixed asset possessions over the past three years. The figures shown in the consolidated balance sheets can be consolidated with those in the statement quite easily, as is shown in Exhibit 25.

Detailed explanations of many of the other balance sheet items are given in a similar fashion. Thus by presenting the essential further information in this way we can achieve a 'cleaner' looking balance sheet layout.

A careful study of the detailed yearly figures relating to the fixed assets will show whether their values are being derived in a consistent fashion. In particular the annual charge for depreciation should be examined in order to ascertain whether

Exhibit 25

For 1973	£000	Explanatory notes for 1973 (Exh.24) £000	Balance Sheet for 1973 (Exh.23) £000
Freeholds total		24,680	24,680
Leaseholds:			
Cost	12,552		
Less: Written off	1,937	10,615	10,615
Plant, etc:			
Cost	43,519		
Less: Written off	20,732	22,787	22,787

For 1974	£000	Explanatory notes for 1974 (Exh.24) £000	Balance Sheet for 1974 (Exh.23) £000
Freeholds total		27,154	27,154
Leaseholds:			
Cost	15,559		
Less: Written off	2,225	13,334	13,334
Plant, etc:			
Cost	51,404		
Less: Written off	24,563	26,841	26,841

1   It appears adequate.
2   It is being calculated in a uniform way.

Now the composition of the depreciation charge for each of the three years 1974, 1973 and 1972 is revealed in Exhibit 24. Here the depreciation sum for the plant and vehicles, etc., is shown on the penultimate line of the statement: the relevant amounts are

      1974   £4,680,000
      1973   £4,139,000
      1972   £4,088,000

Similarly the amortisation charges, i.e. depreciation and loss through passage of time in respect of the leaseholds, are shown on the penultimate line of the leaseholds section of the statement: the relevant amounts are

      1974   £374,000
      1973   £351,000
      1972   £314,000

The summation of these two sets of data comprise the total charges for depreciation levied against the income of each of the three years. In 1974 the total charge was £5,054,000, in 1973 £4,490,000 and in 1972 £4,402,000 and the reader can trace the entry of these amounts in the published profit and loss accounts shown on page 104.

The question of the adequacy of the years' depreciation charges, and of the uniformity of the methods of calculating the various amounts, is a matter of judgement. We do not have any information about the methods used by the Group's accountants to calculate depreciation charges: nor do we know whether these methods are applied fully to all the relevant assets for every year that they are in the Group's possession. However some broad conclusions are possible. When we note that, in Exhibit 24 and in the relevant balance sheets (per Exhibit 25), the book values of plant, etc., are given as

      1974   £51,404,000
      1973   £43,519,000
      1972   £39,784,000

we can see that the depreciation charges for the three years range between 9.1 and 10.2 per cent of the assets' acquisition costs. Even with our incomplete knowledge we can say that the above annual depreciation charges appear reasonable. So far as the leasehold properties are concerned, with their initial outlay costs of

      1974   £15,559,000
      1973   £12,552,000
      1972   £10,641,000

we can assess the average annual amortisation of the leasehold properties to be within the range of 2.4 to 2.9 per cent of these values. Again our knowledge of the detailed mix of lease periods unexpired is not sufficient for a complete appraisal, but the annual depreciation charges appear to be based upon uniform principles and represent a series of acceptable charges.

The charge for depreciation is an important item in the accounting for a business' operations. Two sections of the balance sheet are affected: depreciation is deducted from the acquisition cost (or valuation) of fixed assets; it is also deducted from profit, the residual balance of which appears on the other side of the balance sheet within the Total Shareholders' Interest. Consequently if the depreciation sums for successive years are calculated by different methods, then it is possible that severely fluctuating values for fixed assets and for retained profits will ensue. Here it is important to recognise that such unreasonable fluctuations would limit the worth of year by year comparisons of the firm's performance UNLESS the variations were explained and capable of being taken into account.

Exhibit 26

COURTAULDS LIMITED - WORKING CAPITAL RATIOS

Year	Working capitals £000	Current ratios	Annual* sales £000	Sales per £ of working capital £.
(1)	(2)	(3)	(4)	(5)
1974	317,785	2.10	956,776	3.01
1973	292,505	2.63	777,129	2.66
1972	225,821	2.41	681,488	3.02

*See profit and loss account on page 103 for details of sales

Therefore the 1948 and 1967 Companies Acts specify certain requirements regarding the disclosure — in publish accounts — of the annual depreciation sums which are deducted from asset values in a balance sheet and charged to its accompanying profit and loss account. The legal requirements for disclosure of information in corporate balance sheets and profit and loss accounts are numerous: for ease of reference the relevant provisions of the 1948 and 1967 Companies Acts have been summarised in Chapter 6.

Finally, before leaving the consolidated balance sheets of our two public companies we will examine the Courtaulds Group's increased investment in working capital over the three years. It must be remembered that the worst impacts of a high rate of inflation had not yet affected these accounts as they show the state of the group up to 31 March 1974. Exhibit 26 sets out the relevant features.

Both annual sales and working capital have been increased in 1974 by 40 per cent of the 1972 figures. Furthermore a relatively stable credit worthy position is present by the current ratios in column 3. The group's assets in cash, deposits and debtors is more than enough in each year to cover the current liabilities. Courtauld's credit rating at these times was clearly a very satisfactory one.

Capital employed and capital invested

Now that we have appropriate consolidated balance sheets for the three companies, we can proceed to an analysis of the data given therein. Our main task will be to appraise the asset strength and the financial structure of the Growing Group: the reader can then apply his knowledge to the accounts of the two public companies already referred to.

A study of the Growing Group's assets at year 2 shows that they have increased in (book value) from £725,000 to £1,245,000 (Fixed assets, investments, goodwill £570,000 + current assets £675,000). This growth in wealth is matched by a similar increase in the amount owed by the company (Total long term funds £835,000 + current liabilities £410,000). Thus one of the balance sheet's principal functions is demonstrated — a balancing of the sources of finance with the assets acquired by using that finance. In this comparison the fictitious asset 'Capital Expenses' has been shown as a deduction from the shareholders' interest and NOT shown amongst the company's assets. When the expense is finally written off it will be charged against retained earnings. Showing the £40,000 as a reduction of the figure of shareholders' funds is therefore a proper anticipation of the ultimate action.

Not all of the firm's assets included in the £1,245,000 are being used in its *own operating processes* however: £75,000 realtes to investments in the shares of other companies whilst £35,000 represents the cost of gaining control of its subsidiary X Limited. This latter item ought eventually to be written off by charge to the company's retained earnings. Consequently a case could be sustained for treating the amount in the same way as the capital expenses. But one could also argue that the £35,000 might — in part — describe an undervaluation of X's assets which have been incorporated into the group balance sheet. In whatever way we view the cost of control item and its origin, it does remain as an intangible asset, until written off. This intangible quality will affect the content of some of our ratio comparisons as the succeeding pages will show.

Those tangible fixed and current assets which are available for use in the Growing Group's manufacturing and trading operations have a total *book* value of £1,135,000 (Land, etc. £460,000 + current asset £675,000). Now when corporate profit earning performance comes under scrutiny, the annual profits will be expressed as a percentage of the book value of the assets employed. This ratio is a useful means of comparison with

1 Other businesses of a similar nature.
2 Other periods in the life of the same business.
3 Returns available from, for example, deposits in a building society.

The ratio has its weaknesses because the balance sheet values of assets employed — termed *total capital employed* — will be influenced by the use of different methods of valuing the various assets. Company A might use one method and Company B might use a different method, with consequent variations in asset valuations.* Furthermore when we use the ratio 'return on capital employed' we should be consistent in our interpretation of the term 'return'. This may be defined as, *inter alia,*

Profits, before tax and interest charges
Profits after tax.

Good reasons can be cited for choosing either of these, or other, concepts in appropriate circumstances. We shall discuss the matter repeatedly in subsequent pages but at this point, it is the consistency of method which is being emphasised.

Again the content of the term 'capital employed' can be comprised in several ways. For example, the managers of a business will be concerned in evaluating the results of their operating the firm's principal activities. More precisely they may wish to appraise the performance of the various divisions and sections of the company. For these purposes the concept of capital employed would consist of the total value of the assets *available for use* in the business or division which is being examined. In these instances the value accorded to assets available for use may be

1 The depreciated book value of the tangible fixed assets plus the book value of the current assets *or*
2 The gross, i.e. undepreciated, book value of the tangible fixed

*See L.E. Rockley, *The non-accountant's guide to finance,* pp 45-46, Business Books (1972)

assets plus the book value of the current assets.

But for inter-company comparisons or for an appraisal of returns to *capital invested* in a company, the capital employed concept will be comprised of the book values* of

> Tangible assets available for corporate manufacturing and trading operations
>> *less*
> Current liabilities

Now when this principle is applied to the balance sheet in Exhibit 21, the answer is shown to be £1,135,000 less £410,000, i.e. £725,000. The reasoning behind this particular definition of capital employed recognises that current assets should be regarded as the fund from which the short term (current) liabilities are paid. Therefore the whole of those current assets cannot be presumed to be continuously invested in the company's manufacturing and trading operations. Clearly current assets are constantly changing: raw materials are being converted to goods sold for cash: the cash is used to settle current debts. Therefore it is only the surplus of current assets over current liabilities which can be regarded as capital available for the firm's own operations during the whole trading period. After all when a business is first established, its initial cash needs — the investment sum — will be determined by the cost of the fixed assets *plus* the amount of working capital that would be required to maintain a particular level of trading activity.

Shareholders' capital employed

The Ordinary shareholders view of capital employed is represented by the face value of the total number of Ordinary shares plus the accummulated profits and reserves that have been retained in the company. Profits, and to a large extent reserves, shown in the balance sheet will have arisen from the earnings generated by the firm's profitable business operations in past years. Post-tax profits belong to the proprietors of the company — the shareholders. So far as such profits are not paid to the proprietors in the form of dividends, or not used to finance the issue of bonus shares, they are termed retained earnings. Retained earnings are the additional investments which the residual proprietors (the Ordinary shareholders) have been compelled to leave in the company.

*The writer's repeated references to book values of assets included in these definitions of capital employed will be questioned in a later chapter. The effects of inflation upon the *real* resource values being consumed in business operations must be brought to account. For the moment, however, the fundamental concepts are being explained.

Therefore the Ordinary shareholders' investment in the Growing Group in the two years portrayed in Exhibit 21 is calculated as shown in Exhibit 27.

Exhibit 21 does not show the details of shares in issue: such information would be given as a note to the published accounts but in this instance the reader can verify the actual issued shares from the parent company's balance sheet on pages 41–43. Now the above totals of equity investment should not be confused with the Total Shareholders' Interest which describes the total investment of all shareholders in the company, including the preference shareholdings. The Total Shareholders' Investment for each of the two years was £350,000 and £735,000, respectively.

The amount of the Ordinary shareholders' investment in a company should be compared with the post-tax earnings available for the Ordinary shareholders. When this relationship is expressed in percentage terms, again we have a ratio for comparison between different firms or between different periods in the life of one firm. The reader should note the term 'post-tax earnings *available for the ordinary shareholders.*' Clearly where more than one type of share is in issue, the company's post-tax earnings would not belong wholly to the Ordinary shareholders. Some part of those earnings would be needed to pay the dividends of the Preference shareholders, for example. At this stage we will consider the value of the Total Shareholders' Interest in each of the two public companies, Tesco and Courtaulds. On page 53 the consolidated balance sheet of Courtaulds for 1974 and 1973 sets out the long-term funds of the company — its capital employed or, more appropriately, the capital invested as

	1974 £000	1973 £000
Preference capital	3,479	3,479
Ordinary capital	67,598	67,568
Reserves	284,739	219,781
Relating to Courtaulds Ltd	355,816	290,828
Minority interests	31,446	29,902
Loan capital	268,984	254,382
Deferred taxation	32,427	31,117
	£688,673	£606,229

Now the item 'Relating to Courtaulds Limited: £355,816' would appear to be the 1974 book value of the Total Shareholders' Interest in that company. Clearly, it comprises the nominal value totals of

Exhibit 27   65

BOOK VALUE OF EQUITY INVESTMENT

	Year 1 £	Year 2 £
Issued Ordinary shares	60,000	250,000
Reserves	190,000	435,000*
	£250,000	£685,000

*That is, after deducting capital expenses of £40,000

the issued shares plus the various reserves and as such would normally represent the total book value of the shareholders' investment in any company. Nevertheless we must consider the nature of the 1974 Deferred Taxation sum of £32,427 before making our final judgements of the value of the shareholders' interest. Deferred taxation amounts are comprised of sums which have been charged or set aside from past and current profits. These transfers or charges against profits have been made to account — in the main — for the differences between

1   Charges in the company's profit and loss accounts for depreciation of fixed assets, and
2   The depreciation amount allowed by taxation regulations in respect of those fixed assets.

Now, in general item (2) results in a greater allowance than (1) against the income subject to tax in the earlier years of an asset's life. Such a consequence of the taxation allowances for capital expenditure would have the effect of postponing a firm's potential current taxation liability into subsequent accounting years. Therefore the Deferred Taxation account was devised to offset this action. Transfers from profit and loss account to Deferred Taxation act to bring forward, from those subsequent years, into a current year's account the taxation liabilities which would have been postponed to those later years. But where a company engages in large annual capital expenditure programmes these transfers to the deferred taxation account will grow, as will the size of the deferred taxation account. It becomes difficult to envisage the return of the amounts involved TO the profit and loss account. Certainly no liability by the company to actually pay the deferred taxation sum will arise: the main objective of deferred taxation is merely to achieve a better allocation of the tax charge to individual years.

Many companies do not follow the practice of generating an ever-growing deferred taxation account; they regard the account in the light of a taxation reserve. In such circumstances it would become part of the shareholders' funds invested in the business. Readers must realise however that the authoritative bodies, which establish standard practices for treatment of accounting matters, have ruled that Deferred Taxation should NOT be regarded as part of the Total Shareholders' Interest.

Nevertheless because Courtaulds do NOT follow the practice of making large annual transfers to a growing Deferred Taxation account, we shall include this taxation amount in the calculation of the Total Shareholders' Interest in the company. Its 1974 value then becomes £388,243,000. The comparable figure for Tesco, according to the 1974 balance sheet would be £67,331,000.

So far as the Growing Group is concerned Exhibit 21 coupled with Exhibit 17 shows that the number of Ordinary shares in issue has increased, during year 2, from 60,000 to 250,000. At the same time the book value of the Ordinary shareholders' investment has risen from £250,000 to £685,000. It must be pointed out that these book values of the residual proprietors' investments in the Growing Group include the costs of investments made by the Group in other associated companies. If we were appraising the worth of a holding of one Ordinary share in the Group, then a separate valuation of the corporate investments in other firms would have to be made. With these comments in mind and remembering that the balance sheet values of the fixed assets are derived mostly from their original cost less some equivocal charge for depreciation, the reader can attempt a rough net asset value for one Ordinary share:

Year 1

$$£\frac{250,000 - 68,000}{60,000}$$

$$= £\frac{182,000}{60,000}$$

$$= £3.03$$

Year 2

$$£\frac{685,000 - (75,000 + 35,000)^*}{250,000}$$

$$= £\frac{575,000}{250,000}$$

$$= £2.30$$

*The net book worth of the Ordinary shareholders' Investment in the Growing Group (£685,000) includes the cost of control figure (£35,000) and the cost of quoted and unquoted shares (£75,000) held by the Group. By deducting these sums — which require separate evaluations of worth — we can arrive at a net book worth of the Ordinary shareholders' investment in the corporate tangible assets.

The above asset worths of each Ordinary Share do not take into account the company's

    Investments in associated companies

    Goodwill

    Management ability

    Future profit expectations

The apparent fall in value which has occurred in year 2 does portray one of the problems involved in issuing Ordinary shares. The calculations exemplify a possible impact upon the worth of an existing Ordinary share when the value of that existing equity holding is diluted in consequence of an increase in the number of equity shares in issue. Naturally it would be expected that the enlarged Ordinary shareholders' investment would begin to earn the extra profits necessary to justify the increased amount of equity capital employed. In such an event the asset value of the company would increase and, more importantly, the market price of the shares would reflect the greater earning power of the firm.

Working capital and current ratio

In balance sheet terms, working capital is represented by the book values of the current assets less the book values of the current liabilities. In its most recent balance sheet (page 51) the Growing Group had a working capital of £265,000: in the immediately preceding year the working capital was £32,000. A comparison of these two absolute totals shows that the company's working capital position has improved by £233,000. Now working capital is a measure of the extent to which the current assets could lose their value, before the amounts owing to short-term creditors were jeopardised. Therefore a monthly or an annual trend in the working capital amounts would be a relevant feature to observe in any study of the adequacy of working capital in a company. A matter of even greater significance for corporate liquidity appraisal will be revealed when the *relationship* between assets and current liabilities is quantified. This relationship is called the current ratio, and it is calculated for the most recent balance sheet of the Growing Group as

$$\frac{\text{Current assets}}{\text{Current liabilities}}$$

$$= \frac{675,000}{410,000}$$

$$= 1.65$$

In the previous year the ratio was 1.1. Therefore it is not just the absolute working capital which has increased. The firm's credit worthiness has improved also because for every £1 worth of current liabilities there was £1.65 worth of current assets, *at the date of the last balance sheet.* Thus the value of a ratio, as a convenient means of expressing the relative importances of large sums of money, is demonstrated. Clearly the working capital of £265,000 quoted above could have arisen from current assets of £10,265,000 and current liabilities of £10,000,000. In that case the current ratio would have been 1.03, a more pertinent evaluation of the solvency state which would be evidenced by such current asset and current liability totals.

It is frequently stated that an acceptable current ratio would be 2:1, that is where the value of the current assets is twice the value of the current liabilities. This generally accepted value for the current ratio is a reasonable standard to set, but it should not be regarded as applicable to all firms at all times however. Much will depend on the seasonal nature of the business, the length of the production cycle, general trade conditions and upon the due dates for settlement of the short term liabilities. If most of the Growing Group's short-term liabilities were payable immediately or in the first half of the following month then a ratio of 2:1 might not suffice, unless the majority of the current assets were represented by cash or near cash.

Liquid ratio

Current assets may include stocks of raw materials, work in progress and finished goods, none of which represent guaranteed cash incomes to the company until the final products are actually SOLD. Consequently much subjective judgement may be involved in arriving at the balance sheet values for these (unsold) current assets. A rapid turn-over of current assets would safeguard the company and its short-term creditors from losses due to deteriorating stocks and bad debts. The reader must always remember that the book value of the working capital depends upon valuations accorded to the various types of stock which the company holds. If these are overvalued or if they include unsaleable or unusable commodities, then they would offer no security to the short term creditor. Furthermore, the worth of the business is being overstated. In order therefore to avoid misconceptions which might arise from the use of working capital and current ratio concepts only, it is advisable to calculate the liquid ratio also. This ratio expresses the relationship between the current liabilities and the liquid assets, where the term 'liquid assets' refers to cash, debtors, temporary investments and other short term interest earning deposits.

Using the data given in the Growing Group's most recent balance sheet, the current ratio is derived as follows:

Cash + Debtors (i.e. all current assets except all stocks)
——
Current liabilities

$$= \frac{305,000}{410,000}$$

$$= 0.74$$

The resultant index of 0.74 : 1 means that every £'s worth of current liabilities is covered by only 74p worth of cash and near cash. Now the minimum acceptable level for the liquid ratio would normally be 1 : 1 which would indicate a situation where the total value of the short-term liabilities is just equalled by a similar quantity of liquid assets. It is pointed out however that the above ratio shows the state of affairs as at the date of the last balance sheet. The current state of the firm's finances is more relevant, especially if the firm's business operations are being expanded.

When expansion of business activity takes place additional stocks of raw materials and/other goods will be required. The relationships of liquid assets and current assets to the current liabilities will thus be changed. The change will be most marked where the length of the firm's production and selling cycle is longer than the period of credit allowed by suppliers of the raw materials and other goods. In such circumstances creditors who supplied these goods would have to be paid BEFORE the extra production was able to generate its cash flow. With every successive increase in activity, more expenses for raw materials and other running costs will be incurred. Short-term creditors cannot be expected to wait until the extra business results in higher cash flows. The working capital will be gradually eroded therefore and will have to be restored by the injection of more long-term funds. An issue of shares or debentures becomes necessary.

Working capital analysis

Neither the liquid nor the current ratios can be regarded as complete guides to the ability of a business to meet its current debts. Additional data to assist the analyst in his judgement can be provided by the ratio of cash to current assets. For the balance sheet displayed in Exhibit 21 this ratio would be

$$\frac{45,000}{675,000} = 0.06$$

It is unlikely that such a low ratio would be regarded as satisfactory but more information would be needed before a final conclusion could be made, however. The index merely indicates that some study should be made of the firm's normal cash requirements. A manager could arrive at a reasonable estimate of his normal monthly cash requirements. He would take note of

1 The total wages bill for a period of — say — 6 weeks.
2 The total of the monthly salary payments.
3 An average monthly payments schedule for rent, rates, light, telephone and other running costs.

In this way an estimate of the average monthly cash needs could be produced. When this is compared with the normal current asset holdings, an acceptable ratio can be established. However it has to be remembered that as the level of business activity changes, the need for liquid resources will change also. A complete solvency appraisal cannot be effected by a balance sheet examination only. More information about the trend of business operations is needed. For the company's management a forecast cast budget, being updated by current events, is the only answer.

Also when the ratio of total stocks to net working capital is calculated, the analyst will obtain a clear picture of the impact which a company's stock levels will have upon its working capital and current ratio figures. In the Growing Group's latest balance sheet, the relevant data give the following:

$$\frac{370,000}{265,000} = 1.39$$

A ratio in excess of unity means that the company's stocks are valued at an amount greater than the whole of the working capital. The worth of the stock holdings shown in the balance sheet is 139 per cent of the working capital sum revealed in that balance sheet. Therefore a loss of 10 per cent in the value of these stocks — £37,000 — would result in a 13.9 per cent fall in the book value of the working capital.

If the stock held by the company had been valued at £200,000, then with a similar working capital of £265,000, the ratio would be

$$\frac{200,000}{265,000} = 0.75$$

In this case the various inventories would represent 75 per cent of the working capital. A loss in stock value of 10 per cent, £20,000, would bring a reduction in working capital of 7.5 per cent. These comments are made in order to show that valuations of stock which are large in relation to the book value of working capital, could give that working capital a false rating. If the balance sheet values for company stocks are *less* than 100 per cent of the working capital, then the *whole* of those stocks could be lost without the working capital being completely eliminated. Final judgements about the adequacy and reliability of the working capital, derived from balance sheet figures of current assets and current liabilities, would not be made until the following matters had been examined:

1 Reasons for (overlarge) stockholdings.
2 Growth trends in the company's markets.
3 Size of the company's order book.

Company financing

A company's financial structure is comprised of the share capital reserves, loan stock and other liabilities which form the total funds available for the firm's operations. In this study of company financing we are going to be concerned with the proportion that each of the separate types of finance bear to the whole of the funds available for the firm. As the shareholders are the proprietors of the company, then it is reasonable to expect that they should provide a substantial proportion of the capital supply. This may not always be the case however, especially for those businesses which own many highly valued properties. In these circumstances the company's managers may decide to use more long-term loans than shares to finance their operations. Such loans could be secured against certain of the firm's valuable properties, a form of security which the long-term lender (the debenture holder) seeks in order to protect the capital he invests.*

New Ordinary shares do not carry the right to any fixed rate of dividend. The Ordinary shareholder is the final risk bearer and he might receive a low rate of dividend or a high rate of dividend, depending upon the trading fortunes of the company. On the other hand, the Preference shareholder has a right to a fixed annual rate of dividend, provided that the company has sufficient post-tax profits available to meet the cost of the dividend. Debenture holders are not shareholders and the money value of their loans does not form any part of the Total Shareholders' Interest. Furthermore debenture holders are in a privileged position because they are entitled to a fixed annual rate of interest on their loans to the company. This is an

*Larger loan stock to equity ratios are found also in Finance Companies and Investment Companies.

expense which must be paid in each year whether the firm's operations are profitable or not. The important point about debenture interest is that it is a cost which is charged against income before profit is determined. It therefore acts to reduce the amount of tax payable on corporate profits.

The relationship between fixed interest and fixed dividend financing to total equity financing is called Gearing. Gearing describes the ratio of fixed interest and fixed dividend capital to Ordinary share capital. It is generally expressed by the formula

$$\frac{\text{Preference capital + Long-term debt}}{\text{Equity capital}} \times 100$$

The Growing Group's gearing ratio according to the data for Year 2 in Exhibits 17 and 21 is

$$\frac{50,000 + 100,000}{250,000} \times 100$$

$$= 60\%$$

This low gearing shows that less than half of the Growing Group's long-term capital is of the fixed reward type. Moreover an examination of the Group's consolidated balance sheet reveals an adequate quantity of tangible fixed assets which offer security for the loan capital (provided the assets are not over valued).

In comparison Tesco has comparatively few loan stocks in issue and no preference shares at all (pages 54 and 55): therefore its financial structure is a very low geared one. But Courtaulds is a highly geared company as the balance sheets on pages 44 and 53 will demonstrate. Data taken from the consolidated balance sheet (page 53) enables us to calculate Courtauld's gearing ratios for the three years 1974, 1973 and 1972, as shown below:

$$\frac{\text{Preference capital + Loan capital}}{\text{Ordinary capital}} \times 100$$

$$\text{in 1974} = \frac{3479 + 268984}{67598} \times 100 = 403\%$$

$$\text{in 1973} = \frac{3479 + 254382}{67568} \times 100 = 382\%$$

$$\text{in 1972} = \frac{3479 + 219150}{67460} \times 100 = 330\%$$

These ratios indicate a steadily increasing reliance by Courtaulds
Limited on borrowed capital rather than share capital, during the
three-year period. Nevertheless there appears to be a sufficiency of
fixed assets in the group's balance sheet to act as security for the loan
capital — should that security be really needed. Indeed if we express
the loan capital as a percentage of the book values for land, buildings,
plant and equipment, in each year, we shall obtain a better picture.
The relevant percentages are

1974	76%
1973	85%
1972	76%

From this analysis of the changes in the group's long-term financing
we can see that even though the gearing ratio has increased markedly,
the cover for the loans (many are unsecured as the notes to the
accounts reveal) in the form of capital assets has not been reduced.
It may be said that the increased borrowing has financed a large
proportion of the asset growth. Much of the loan stock is serviced
by comparatively low rates of interest and therefore would not be
regarded as an unacceptable burden, particularly in view of Courtaulds excellent trading profits.

Effects of gearing

Ezra Solomon has suggested that company managers should aim to
at least maintain the value of the proprietors' interest in the firm.*
Generally this objective will be met where the market price of the
Ordinary shares does not fall in relation to other companies' shares.
But the market value of a company's Ordinary shares is influenced
by many factors, and one of the most effective of these influences is
the maintainable post-tax profits which are expected to be available
to the Ordinary shareholder, in the future. Debenture Capital has a
low post-tax cost. Therefore the more that a company's operations
are financed in this way, the greater will be the post-tax profits
available for the ordinaries. In consequence there will be a tendency
for the market value of the Ordinary shares to stand at a higher
rather than a lower price. The following Exhibits have been designed
to highlight the effect of loan stock and preference share financing
upon the corporate post-tax profits available for Ordinary shares.
Three separate financing structures are postulated, where the interest

*E. Solomon, *The theory of financial management*, Columbia University Press
(1963)

Exhibit 28

CORPORATE FINANCING

Type of finance	Firm A £	Firm B £	Firm C £
10% Debentures	100,000	50,000	–
8% Preference shares	50,000	50,000	50,000
Ordinary shares	50,000	100,000	150,000
Gearing ratio	300%	100%	$33^1/_3\%$
Gearing level	High	Medium	Low

or dividend rates are given, in Exhibit 28. The three firms A, B and C are committed to the payment of rewards to varying levels of prior capital before the Ordinary shareholder can receive any dividend at all. In firm A the prior capital — so-called because it receives its interest/ dividend payments in priority to the Ordinary shareholders — is comprised of

£100,000 of debentures : interest due at 10% = £10,000 p.a.
£50,000 preference shares : dividend due at 8% = £4,000 p.a.

Similarly Firm B can be expected to pay in each year £5,000 interest to its debenture holders and £4,000 dividend to the Preference shareholders. Firm C has a prior capital commitment of £4,000 dividend to its preference shareholders only.

Now to demonstrate the potential effects upon Ordinary share prices of the above interest/dividend requirements for the prior capital, two different levels of profit are suggested for each company. Exhibit 29 shows how the expected profits available for each ordinary share will vary with each of the differently structured companies. Here it is important to realise that the variations in earnings, belonging to ONE Ordinary share, arise solely as a result of the capital gearing. The reader will observe that interest payable on debentures is charged against profits before the taxation amount is calculated. On the other hand, dividends to all kinds of shares are paid out of profits which have suffered tax.

The effect of high gearing is clearly shown: the higher the profits the greater will be the relative share of earnings available for each one of the Ordinary shares in issue. Such a situation would be expected to result in a higher share price for the Ordinary shares of Company A than for the Ordinary shares of companies B and C. It has to be remembered however that the burden of the fixed interest/dividend

Exhibit 29

EARNINGS AVAILABLE FOR ORDINARIES

Details	Firm A	Firm B	Firm C
1 Number of Ordinary shares in issue	50,000	100,000	150,000
2	£	£	£
Profits before tax and interest	20,000	20,000	20,000
Less Debenture interest	10,000	5,000	-
Profits before tax	10,000	15,000	20,000
Corporation Tax at 50%	5,000	7,500	10,000
Profits after tax	5,000	7,500	10,000
Less Preference dividend	4,000	4,000	4,000
Available for Ordinaries	£1,000	£3,500	£6,000
Earnings per one Ordinary share	2p	3.5p	4p
3	£	£	£
Profits before tax and interest	50,000	50,000	50,000
Less Debenture interest	10,000	5,000	-
Profits before tax	40,000	45,000	50,000
Corporation Tax at 50%	20,000	22,500	25,000
Profits after tax	20,000	22,500	25,000
Less Preference dividend	4,000	4,000	4,000
Available for Ordinaries	£16,000	£18,500	£21,000
Earnings per one Ordinary share	32p	18.5p	14p

requirements of the prior capital suppliers creates problems for low-profit companies. Firm A, at the profit level of £20,000 is a good example of this situation. Thus an Ordinary shareholding in a highly geared low-profit company such as Firm A becomes less attractive than a similar holding in a low-geared low-profit company such as Company C at the profit level of £20,000. Gearing can produce widely fluctuating earnings per Ordinary share, and consequently potentially wide variations in the Ordinary dividends also. Companies whose shares experience *wide* variations in dividends and earnings, from one year to another, do not normally enjoy a high rating on the Stock Exchange.

All forms of corporate finance have a cost. An Ordinary shareholder must receive some return on his investment, otherwise the market value of his holding will fall. When a company's ordinary shares fall in price on the Stock Exchange, it becomes more expensive for the company to finance its replacements, diversification and modernisation, in this way*. Therefore a financing strategy has to balance the benefits of fixed low-interest, low-dividend capitals against the higher return expectations of the equity shareholder. The policy to be adopted must have regard to the requirements of the different classes of investor, *and* the ability of the company to meet these requirements. It is emphasised that debenture issues should not be recommended where

1　The company's business is of a speculative nature.
2　The company's profits are liable to considerable fluctuations.
3　The company is in the early stages of establishing itself on a sound profit making basis.

A steady reliable profit-making performance would be a principal criterion for a company to satisfy before making such an issue. Other facts relevant to an issue of loan stock are that the company should have

1　A sufficiency of long-term assets to act as security for the eventual return of the capital sum to the lenders.
2　A sufficiency of current income to ensure the payment in each year of the debenture interest.

Finally it must be pointed out that a company's capital gearing cannot be changed very rapidly. It is only when a new supply of long-term capital money is to be sought, that the gearing ratio can be

---

*A direct result of the fall in share price would be that more shares would have to be issued in order to obtain a specific sum of money. Moreover a larger issue coupled with a lower (or falling) share price could portend as unsuccessful issue i.e. a situation where many of the shares are not taken up by the investing public. Thus underwriting costs and other expenses of issue could rise sharply. An equity issue made in such circumstances becomes too expensive.

varied. Thus corporate capital planning is a long-term concept: a thorough examination of the firm's future profit expectations, as well as its asset strengths, will have to be undertaken in order to determine the best mix of capital funds for the type of business which the firm envisages.

The shareholders' investment in the company

Other capital structure ratios demonstrate the relative importance of the different types of funds being used by a company. The first of these comparisons will show the proportion that issued loan stock bears to the whole of the corporate long-term finance:

$$\frac{\text{Long-term loans}}{\text{Paid-up capital + Long-term loans}} \times 100$$

$$= \frac{100,000 \times 100}{400,000}$$

$$= 25\%$$

The above ratio has been calculated from the information given in Exhibit 21 for year 2 of the Growing Group. It shows that one quarter of the 'permanent' capital of the company has been provided by long-term *lenders* of funds, such as the debenture holders. In this sense the ratio is similar in its emphasis to the concept of gearing. Whether the above percentage should or should not be regarded as too high will depend upon the nature of the company's business, its profits and its asset structure. But 25 per cent is an acceptable rating for the average business, provided that the strictures listed in the previous section are observed. The reader should note that the Growing Group's loan stock ratio in year 1 was 23.8 per cent. It could be concluded therefore, that the longer term financing strategy, which the company's directorate was envisaging, involves a proportion of loan stock financing of about 25 per cent.

So far the analysis of the Growing Group's capital structure has been concerned with comparisons of the shares and loan stock in issue. But the total supply of funds includes the whole of the shareholders' investment, i.e. the reserves also, plus loan stock plus the current liabilities. The amount of credit provided by short term lenders is given by the quantity of the current debts owed by the firm. Therefore in order to present a more comprehensive picture of the Group's financing practices the following ratios have been calculated. The data are taken from Exhibit 21.

1 *Ratio of Liabilities to the Total Shareholders' Interest*

$$= \frac{\text{Long-term loans + Current liabilities}}{\text{Total shareholders' interest}} \times 100$$

$$= \frac{100,000 + 410,000}{735,000} \times 100$$

$$= 69.4\%$$

2 *Ratio of Current Liabilities to Total Long-term Funds*

$$= \frac{\text{Current liabilities}}{\text{Total shareholders' interest + Long-term loans}} \times 100$$

$$= \frac{410,000}{735,000 + 100,000} \times 100$$

$$= 49\%$$

A rise in either of these two percentages would suggest a need for examination. Increases in the ratio percentages would show that the shareholders were contributing a lower proportion of the capital required to operate the company. Whilst this may not by itself be a matter for criticism, the ability of the firm eventually to liquidate such increasing amounts of external debt should be kept under review. In these matters the analyst will be interested in the trend of the ratio percentages derived from the data of several years' balance sheets and trading conditions. Moreover different industries will require and will enable different financing strategies: thus the analyst will condition his conclusions by reference to these other material factors which will have their influences upon corporate financing. Nevertheless a growing quantity of current liabilities (in relation to other funds) could be stimulated by over-trading. The short-term creditors would be shown to be financing a permanent growth of corporate operations. A trend towards over-trading must be arrested before the short-term creditors lose faith in the ability and willingness of the firm to settle its current debts promptly, or at all! Additional supplies of *long-term* finance would be needed.

A final measure of the proprietors' investment will now be studied

$$= \frac{\text{Total shareholders' interest}}{\text{Book value of the fixed assets}} \times 100$$

$$= \frac{735,000}{460,000} \times 100$$

$$= 160\%$$

Again the data are taken from Exhibit 21. The ratio shows that the shareholders' funds are not invested in fixed assets only but in working capital and in the shares of associated companies also. If the reader examines the Group's balance sheet for the previous year, then comparable values for the above three ratios can be obtained. These previous year's ratios were 107, 81 and 116 per cent, respectively. The conclusions to be drawn from this information are that (a) the proprietors have properly assumed a greater relative responsibility for the company's financing (ratio 1): (b) the reliance placed upon short-term funds has been reduced in favour of longer term finance (ratio 2): and (c) the proprietors' investment is not confined to the book value of the fixed assets but is being spread more widely over the firm's possessions (ratio 3).

Courtaulds and Tesco

Exhibits 30 and 31 show how the balance sheets of Tesco and Court-aulds (pages 53 — 55) can be used to calculate similar ratios which will highlight the relative proportions of shareholders' funds and other funds invested in those businesses. Ratio 1 in each of the two exhibits demonstrates that the asset growths of both companies are being financed more by the other liabilities (Loan stock and current liabilities) than by shareholders' funds. It should be observed that whilst the *rate* of change is more marked for Tesco than for Court-aulds, the former group's combination of sources of funds has only recently attained a 50/50 mix.

Ratio 2 in both companies gives added emphasis to the implications already noted in that the proportions of current liabilities are growing noticeably. Here the special position of supermarkets, and particularly of Tesco, is revealed: the data trend in this group is influenced by

1   An almost complete lack of gearing.
2   The financing of current selling operations by current liabilities
     (a rapid stock turnover accompanied by a wholly cash trade).
On the other hand Courtaulds ratios reflect what we already know —

Exhibit 30

SHAREHOLDERS' INVESTMENTS

Ratio	COURTAULDS GROUP		
	1974	1973	1972
1 Liabilities to Total Shareholders' Interest	$\dfrac{268984 + 287692}{388243} \times 100$ = 143%	$\dfrac{254382 + 179325}{321945} \times 100$ = 135%	$\dfrac{219150 + 159865}{282654} \times 100$ = 134%
2 Current Liabilities to Long-term Funds	$\dfrac{287692}{388243 + 268984} \times 100$ = 44%	$\dfrac{179325}{321945 + 254382} \times 100$ = 31%	$\dfrac{159865}{282654 + 219150} \times 100$ = 32%
3 Total Shareholders' Interest to Fixed Assets	$\dfrac{388243}{354161} \times 100$ = 110%	$\dfrac{321945}{300377} \times 100$ = 107%	$\dfrac{282654}{290097} \times 100$ = 97%

Exhibit 31

SHAREHOLDERS' INVESTMENTS

Ratio	TESCO GROUP		
	1974	1973	1972
1 Liabilities to Total Shareholders' Interest	$\dfrac{546 + 59673 + 8873}{68331} \times 100$ $= 101\%$	$\dfrac{609 + 42238 + 8010}{57808} \times 100$ $= 88\%$	$\dfrac{647 + 31538 + 5522}{48314} \times 100$ $= 78\%$
2 Current Liabilities to Long-term Funds	$\dfrac{59673 + 8873}{68331 + 546} \times 100$ $= 100\%$	$\dfrac{42238 + 8010}{57808 + 609} \times 100$ $= 86\%$	$\dfrac{31538 + 5522}{48314 + 647} \times 100$ $= 76\%$
3 Total Shareholders' Interest to Fixed Assets	$\dfrac{68331}{67329} \times 100$ $= 101\%$	$\dfrac{57808}{58082} \times 100$ $= 100\%$	$\dfrac{48314}{53925} \times 100$ $= 90\%$

the group had a strong liquid position at March 1974 as its then working capital and current ratios show (page 60).

Ratio 3 tells us that, for both groups, the extent to which shareholders' funds are invested in fixed assets is very much the same. With regard to Courtaulds we have already seen (pages 72/3) how the increased gearing of the group will have assisted in financing its asset growth. Exhibit 30 gives further support to those conclusions.

When we look for reasons behind these changes in corporate financing, we must turn to an examination of the fixed and current asset structures of the two groups. Appropriate data is given in Exhibit 32.

Clearly the proportion of current assets in the total assets mixes has grown year by year. This reflects increased costs of financing stocks and debtors in a period of rising prices. To some extent also the changes in the weight of current assets will be due to the increased output performance of these two reputable companies. One would expect, in these circumstances, a good measure of current assets growth to be financed by short-term financing, a point demonstrated in Exhibits 30 and 31.

Exhibit 32

FIXED AND CURRENT ASSET PROPORTIONS

Asset type	COURTAULDS					
	1974		1973		1972	
	£000	%	£000	%	£000	%
Fixed	354161	36.9	300377	38.9	290097	42.9
Current	605477	63.1	471830	61.1	385686	57.1
Total of both	959638	100.0	772207	100.0	675783	100.0

Asset type	TESCO					
	1974		1973		1972	
	£000	%	£000	%	£000	%
Fixed	67329	50.5	58082	53.5	53925	62.7
Current	65907	49.5	50573	46.5	32093	37.3
Total of both	133236	100.0	108655	100.0	86018	100.0

The ratios dealt with in this publication derive from the relationships existing between two variables. These comparisons do not of themselves create business activity. They merely show how in simple form, the company managements can be supplied with data about developments in their firm's trading and financing operations. This kind of information is available to anyone who is prepared to study the balance sheets and other statements which are published, year after year, by limited companies in the U.K.

It is not suggested that a long list of ratios must *always* be compiled, either for corporate management purposes or for investigations carried out by other interested parties. The studies to be undertaken will be determined to some extent by the importance of the enquiry and by the needs of the investigators for certain special information. Many business directorates maintain an effective control over their operating units by using only five or six principal ratios as guidelines about their firm's progress. This aspect of corporate management will be discussed in a later chapter.

Further reading

R.J. Chambers, *Financial management,* Law Book Company, (1967). (See especially Chapters 11-15).

F.P. Langley, *Introduction to accounting for business studies,* Butterworths (1970). (See especially Chapters 1, 2, 4 and 16).

W.T. Baxter and S. Davidson, *Studies in accounting theory,* Sweet & Maxwell (1962). (See especially sections on 'Concepts of Depreciation' and 'Depreciation — to measure income or provide funds for replacement'.).

L.E. Rockley, *The non-accountant's guide to finance,* Business Books (1972).

S.H. Archer and C.A. D'Ambrosio, *Business finance: theory and management,* Macmillan (1972). (See especially Parts I and V, and Chapter 25).

G.A. Holmes, 'Capital gearing', *Accountancy,* pp 930-32 (December 1969).

C.R. Tomkins, 'The development of relevant published accounting reports, *ibid.,* pp 815-20 (November 1969).

3 | *Funds Flow and Profits*

Introduction

The previous chapters have shown how the information given in a company's balance sheet can be used to reveal some of the strengths and weaknesses of that company. There is a limit however to the usefulness of a single statement. Therefore if we wish to pursue our analysis of corporate worth, we shall have to study the profit and loss account also. This is essential because the balance sheet presents a picture of the firm on a particular day *only*, the date at the head of the statement. What it does not show is how the business has used its assets since the date of the previous balance sheet, to enable it to reach the state of affairs currently being revealed.

The profit and loss account

If we wish to identify those corporate worth changes which have arisen as a result of the firm's trading activities over a period of time,

Exhibit 33 85

THE GROWING COMPANY LIMITED

Profit and loss account for the year ended....

Expenditure	*Income*
Entries on this side of the account show the value of the *input*: the cost of goods and services *consumed*, during the period given above, to obtain the income shown on the other side of the account	Entries on this side of the account show the value of the *output*: the income *receivable* during the period given above, as a result of using the goods and services listed on the other side of the account

then the profit and loss account is the statement to examine. A profit and loss account (also known as the revenue account, the income and expenditure account or the income account) summarises the revenue incomes and expenditures of the business *over a period*. That period is given at the head of the statement in the description 'Profit and Loss Account for the Year ended 31 December 19. .', as in Exhibit 33.

Two important characteristics of the profit and loss account must be appreciated, at this stage. The account reflects only

1 *Revenue items:* these refer to the day to day running costs and incomes of the business: no long term values or acquisitions are involved, for the account is designed to show the results of trading* - a comparison of the costs of an input (wages, salaries, materials used, etc.) against the value of an output (sales) produced by business activity.

2 *Incomes and expenditures:* the profit and loss account records, for the period shown at the head of the account

   (a) the cost of, i.e. the expenditure on, goods and services consumed during that period to generate the sales of the period:

*The reader will encounter instances where a profit and loss account shows profits and losses of a capital nature, i.e. not resulting from the company's normal trading activities. These items have to be ignored when appraising a firm's *trading* profitability, which the profit and loss account is expected to show.

(b) the value of the output sold, i.e. the income, of the period. Profit and loss accounts are not designed, nor are they expected to show, the amounts of money paid or received during an accounting period. Such movements of cash are itemised in the cash account where they are termed receipts and payments.

Nevertheless, most of the items in a PL account will eventually result in cash movement. When payment is made for wages, salaries and materials, cash will flow *from* the business. The relevant amounts will then be shown in the cash book. Similarly when the company's customers pay for the goods they have bought, cash will flow *to* the business, and again the relevant amounts will be shown in the cash account. Thus if the value of the sales is greater than the costs of goods consumed in obtaining those sales, not only will the firm make a profit but a net flow of cash INTO the firm will be generated. Exhibit 34 presents a simple example to demonstrate this point.

Clearly when payments are made for the materials and other services which the business has consumed, then £800 will flow from the corporate treasury. On the other hand when the firm's customers pay for the goods sold to them, then £1,000 will flow into the corporate treasury. The result of these transactions will be a net cash inflow, to the company, of £200. Thus profit and cash generation would appear to be the same, but rarely does this happen in fact. The principal reason for differences between profit and cash flow stems from the terms of trade (credit) which businesses give and receive. In view of such credit trading all of the actual cash account entries will not match with all of the PL account entries. Some of the cash movements will not take place until after the end of the PL account period in which the relevant expenditures and incomes are recorded.

Exhibit 34

Profit and loss account for the year ended....

Expenditure	£	Income	£
Materials	300	Sales	1,000
Wages	200		
Salaries	250		
Rent	50		
Profit	200		
	£1,000		£1,000

Now an important item of expenditure for a manufacturing or trading business will be the acquisition costs of its fixed assets. These are the company's capital expenditures: they include such things as buildings, plant, machinery and equipment, and they are listed in the balance sheet. Cash payments for these goods will be made when they are acquired or at least shortly after acquisition. But it would be completely unrealistic to list the whole amount of such expenditures in that PL account relating to the year during which the fixed assets were purchased. This is because capital assets are expected to last longer than one profit period: it is not intended that they should be entirely consumed in earning the income shown in a *single year's* PL account. Therefore the cost (either the historic, acquisition cost or the revalued 'cost') of fixed assets is spread over several years in order to charge against the income of each of those years a portion of the fixed asset expenditure. A more complete version of the costs of earning income is recorded and hence a more realistic profit is determined. The allocation of the costs of fixed assets to the several PL accounts compiled during the asset's economic lives, is called 'depreciation'.

It is now proposed to revise the PL account shown in Exhibit 34 by bringing to the account a charge for depreciation — a 'cost of use' of corporate fixed assets—see Exhibit 35. The item for depreciation is the period's allocation of the original outlay cost of fixed assets. These assets may well have been paid for several years ago. Clearly therefore the entry for depreciation does not indicate the movement of a particular cash sum: no payment for depreciation will be found

Exhibit 35

Profit and loss account for the year ended....

Expenditure	£	Income	£
Materials	300	Sales	1,000
Wages	200		
Salaries	250		
Rent	50		
Depreciation	100		
Profit	100		
	£1,000		£1,000

in any cash book. Consequently the appearance in a PL account of expenditure items called depreciation will have NO effect upon the cash flow generated by trading operations. That flow will still be £200 for the account shown in Exhibit 35, as it was for Exhibit 34. In the light of this explanation we can redefine 'cash flow' as profit plus depreciation, i.e. £100 + £100 = £200, though this particular sum must be termed more precisely as the *gross* cash flow generated by trading operations.

Net cash flows and corporate growth

If it is now assumed that tax at the rate of 50 per cent is charged on the declared profits of £100, then the company's net earnings, i.e. profits after tax, will be shown as in Exhibit 36. Here the operating profit, previously shown to be £100, is reduced by the amount due to be paid by the company in respect of its taxation liability. Previously, Exhibits 34 and 35 have shown that £800 would eventually have to be paid for the goods and services consumed in achieving sales of £1,000. The taxation charge will result in the cash out flows being raised from £800 to £850 and thus the post-tax cash flow from operations becomes £150. These post-tax cash flows are termed *net* cash flows and can be described as post-tax profits plus depreciation (£50 + £100).

As cash is generated by the company's profitable trading, some of this money will be used to buy new fixed assets and replace old ones. Furthermore if the firm's current business is expanding or if new products are being developed, more cash will have to be invested in greater stockholdings. Larger stocks of raw materials and finished goods will be necessary to service the demands of the increased trade. Again buoyant trading conditions which lead to expanding sales — in both value and volume — will entail a greater investment in debtors. For these reasons any increase in the net cash flows will not be reflected permanently in the company's cash resources. We could not assume that the net cash flows of £150 revealed in Exhibit 36 would result in the company's cash balance being £150 greater at the end of the year than it was at the beginning thereof. Nevertheless such comments do not detract from the importance of the concept of net cash flow from operations, or from the calculations which have been used above to demonstrate its potential size. It must be remembered that, where a business calls forth additional investments in fixed assets or stocks or debtors, the investment has to be financed. Without a substantial cash flow *internally generated*, then more outside funds will have to be obtained — such as an issue of shares, or debentures

Exhibit 36   89

Profit and loss account for the year ended....

Expenditure	£	Income	£
Materials	300	Sales	1,000
Wages	200		
Salaries	250		
Rent	50		
Depreciation	100		
Profit before tax	100		
	£1,000		£1,000
Tax	50	Profit before tax	100
Profit after tax	50		
	£100		£100

Exhibit 37
FUNDS FLOW

External funds, sales of corporate assets

1 Creditors
6 Cash
2 Stock of raw materials
7 'Cash flow' (profit)
5 Debtors
3 Work in progress
4 Finished goods
8 Expenditure on fixed assets
9 Increase in working capital

Exhibit 38

THE GROWING COMPANY LIMITED AND ITS SUBSIDIARY

Consolidated Profit and Loss Accounts for the
years ended...

	Year 1		Year 2	
	£000	£000	£000	£000
Sales		1,500		3,000
Less Cost of sales		1,100		2,000
Gross profit		400		1,000
Add Income from investments		5		10
		405		1,010
Less Debenture interest	3		6	
Admin. etc. expenses	362	365	904	910
Profit before tax		40		100
Tax		20		35
Profit after tax		20		65
Add Balance B/F from previous year		11		15
Available for appropriation		31		80
Less Preference dividend	6		3	
Ordinary dividend	5		25	
Transfer to reserve	5	16	17	45
Balance to Balance Sheet		£15		£35

or the negotiation of a bank overdraft.

(It does not need an expanding trade situation to absorb the corporate net cash flow. If there are more stocks and debtors at the end of a period's trading than at the beginning of that period, then without an injection of fresh capital money, the net cash flow would have been used to finance the additional investment in working capital. This can happen without an increase in trade — it will arise due to the impact of inflation upon rising costs of raw material stocks, work-in-progress, etc.)

Exhibit 37 demonstrates the relationships between net cash flow from operations, external funds and expenditures on fixed assets and working capital.

Narrative and consolidated profit and loss accounts

The PL accounts given above have been drawn on conventional two-sided form. But these accounts can be shown in narrative form also, a method of presentation which has been displayed already in the construction of balance sheets. There are various styles of narrative PL account and the details of their content may well vary. In particular the reader must realise that the published PL accounts of limited companies — which are drawn mostly in narrative form — merely give the information which is required by the various Companies Acts.

The ready understanding which a narrative form of accounts encourages, plus the fact that most published accounts are shown in this form, demands that the narrative layout will be used in the forthcoming PL account exhibits. Moreover these examples will be described as 'Consolidated' or 'Group' PL accounts because they will, similar to the consolidated balance sheets, incorporate appropriate proportions of the profits or losses of the subsidiary companies. Hence our studies will proceed to an examination of the data included in the Growing Group's Consolidated Profit and Loss Account, (see Exhibit 38) and in the published accounts of certain public limited companies also.

Concealed within the abbreviated expenditure narrations of the two accounts in Exhibit 38, will be the respective annual charges for depreciation. So let it be assumed that the detailed charges for fixed asset depreciation, which are included in the above profit and loss accounts, are as follows:

	Year 1 £	Year 2 £
Land and buildings	15,000	15,000
Plant	10,000	20,000
Vehicles	8,000	10,000
Equipment	2,000	2,000
Totals	£35,000	£47,000

Armed with this additional information the reader will now be able to calculate the operating cash flows of the company for each of the two years. Exhibit 39 gives these calculations and it should be noted that the term 'operating cash flows' should describe the cash flows generated by trading operations. Investment incomes and costs of capital funds, e.g. interest on debentures, not being purely trading incomes and expenditures, should be excluded.

Clearly the Growing Group is using its increased asset worth in an effective fashion. But when appraising the adequacy of a particular cash flow amount, we have to examine the corporate needs for cash. We have to judge whether the company can generate and/or acquire sufficient finance to maintain and develop its trading activities, modernise its plant and equipment and extend its manufacturing units. A certain amount of relevant information is provided in the published accounts, for the 1948 and 1967 Companies Acts require that registered limited companies must disclose details of

1   Capital expenditures authorised by the directors but not, at the date of the balance sheet, contracted for.

2   Aggregate or estimated amounts of contracts for authorised capital expenditure where such amounts have not, at the date of the balance sheet, been provided for in the accounts.

A comparison of the trend of net cash flows, and particularly of the current year's net cash flow, will show whether the company will be able to finance these capital expenditures from internal funds – or whether it will have to do one of the following:

1   Go to the market for more funds, i.e. shares or loan stock.

2   Secure overdraft facilities at the bank.

Each of these two propositions will interest various people who have business relationships with the company. Shareholders may be concerned at the dilution of their proprietorial interest unless any new share issue was accomplished by a rights issue. Again short-term creditors might be concerned to see the company's liquidity status deteriorate, unless they took the view that the expansion plans presaged increasing business opportunities.

Securing an adequate cash flow from trading operations becomes even more important in a period of inflation. During a time of rapidly rising prices more and more finance has to be invested in materials, work-in-progress, finished goods and debtors. The capital expenditures referred to above will also have to be financed. Thus whilst it may be said that the existence of a credit balance on a firm's profit and loss account *must* indicate a positive cash flow from trading, at the same time the company can be experiencing liquidity problems. These circumstances will arise when a considerable proportion of the corporate cash flow is being absorbed by the increasing costs of normal business operations.

A more realistic strategy of sales pricing or cost reductions becomes

Exhibit 39

COMPARATIVE CASH FLOWS

Details	Gross cash flows			Net cash flows		
	Year 1	Year 2	+	Year 1	Year 2	+
	£000	£000	£000	£000	£000	£000
Depreciation charged during the year	35	47	+12	35	47	+12
Trading profits before tax	38*	96	+58	-	-	-
Trading profits after tax				18	61	+43
Total flows	£73	£143	+£70	£53	£108	+£55

*Derived from gross profit of £400 less administration expenses of £362

necessary. Longer term cash planning has to be linked with short-term cash budgeting. Even so these plans and strategies will be conditioned by the severity of the competition from other firms in the company's line of business, and from other products which may be regarded as acceptable substitutes.

Fund flow statements

Source and application of funds

A complete analysis of a company's financing strategy will be revealed by a study of several Funds Flow Statements, which study can be derived from a sequence of the firm's published accounts. A Funds Flow Statement will also show management how their cash and credit has been used during the operating period which runs from one balance sheet date to the next.

Before we study these documents however, the term 'funds flow' itself must be examined in order to clarify the object of our study. Cash flows have been defined as those money flows which are generated by the firm's own trading operations. Here the cash consequences of manufacturing trading and selling were quantified.

Funds flow connotes a wider view of corporate money management. In this context the term 'funds' refers to the whole supply of money and credit which the firm uses to enable it to carry on its business. Immediately the reader should think of

Shares
Cash flows
Debentures
Loans
Bank overdraft
Short-term credit
Sales of assets

in order to embrace the breadth of the term 'funds'. Noticeably the concept of funds flow is not just concerned with the flow of *capital money* into the firm. Credit facilities and overdrafts must be brought into the picture also, in order to ascertain fully how the company was able to operate its capital and revenue transactions during the period to which the Funds Flow Statement refers.

These statements are compiled in various ways. The reason for the different presentations of Fund Flow Statements stems from different interpretations of the term 'funds'. Furthermore a Funds Flow Statement can be constructed to present certain information in sharp outline: thus we can show

1   A complete list of all the sources of funds and its comparison with a complete list of the uses to which those funds were put.
2   How the sources and uses of funds have affected the company's working capital.
3   How the sources and uses of funds have affected the company's cash balances.
4   The extent to which corporate *growth* is being financed by long term capital money rather than by short-term creditors.

The object of any funds flow statement is to show how a firm's asset/liability status has changed during a specified period – normally one year. Thus the information given in two balance sheets will contain the basic data for calculating the details which are to be listed in the funds flow statement. Exhibit 40 below shows how such basic data comparisons should be set out. The information has been taken from the Growing Group's balance sheet in Exhibit 21. The comparative statement repeats the values given in the year 1 and year 2 balance sheets and cites the variations which occurred during the intervening year.

Now the reader will realise that any increase during the year in the value of an asset, or the appearance of a new asset in the second balance sheet, indicates an application of the firm's funds. The firm's

Exhibit 40

THE GROWING GROUP

Comparative Statement

	Year 1	Year 2	Application of funds +	Source of funds −
	£	£	£	£
ASSETS				
Cost of control	–	35,000	35,000	–
Land, buildings, plant, equipment, and vehicles	300,000	460,000	160,000	–
Investments	68,000	75,000	7,000	–
Stocks	252,000	370,000	118,000	–
Debtors	101,000	260,000	159,000	–
Bank and cash	4,000	45,000	41,000	–
Capital expenses	–	40,000	40,000	–
	£725,000	£1,285,000	£560,000	–

	Year 1	Year 2	Source of funds +	Application of funds −
	£	£	£	£
LIABILITIES				
Share capital	160,000	300,000	140,000	–
Reserves	190,000	475,000	285,000	
Loan capital	50,000	100,000	50,000	
Creditors and accrued expenses	190,000	285,000	95,000	
Taxation	35,000	55,000	20,000	
Bills payable	25,000	70,000	45,000	
Bank overdraft	75,000	–	–	75,000
	£725,000	£1,285,000	£635,000	£75,000

possessions have grown in monetary size: an additional investment in that asset has been made. One exception to this statement refers to assets which are revalued. Here book values are revised to give a more realistic worth for the items involved but *no funds transfer will have taken place.*

Conversely we can say that any decrease in the value of an asset must indicate a source of funds. An asset has been sold or scrapped, though it may be that the actual receipts will have to be separately calculated. If we now turn to the liabilities and calculate the variations in these items, we can ascertain other sources of funds. Where liabilities are shown to have increased, then such increases reveal sources of funds. A decrease in liabilities will, on the other hand, demonstrate an application of funds, in that some debt has been redeemed.

The comparative statement in Exhibit 40 is the result of a simple arithmetical exercise. It can be proved in total before proceeding to the preparation of a specific Funds Flow Statement. But it is pointed out that the details in the comparative statement are very limited: this is because Exhibit 21 is presented in an abbreviated form, as are most published balance sheets. Further information on share capital, fixed assets would have to be sought from the explanatory notes which accompany the published accounts. A greater amount of detail about the year's changes in the corporate wealth would then be available for the Funds Flow Statement.

Source and application of funds

A Funds Flow Statement (Exhibit 41) can now be prepared by using the figures given in the final two columns of Exhibit 40. They give data about the changes which have occurred in the Growing Group's assets and liabilities during year 2.

With one exception, every item in the Funds Flow Statement of Exhibit 41 can be traced from the balance sheet comparisons presented in Exhibit 40. The additional item which appears in Exhibit 41 refers to depreciation. Now the reader will recall that, when the concept of operational cash flows was studied, it was emphasised that the depreciation charges listed in a profit and loss account must be added to the profits after tax in order to arrive at the corporate net cash flows.

Furthermore it has been explained that General Reserves are created out of the corporate profits after tax. Therefore, to ascertain a company's net operating cash flow from a comparison of two successive balance sheets, it will be necessary to aggregate

1   The increase in general reserves.
2   The increase in the profit and loss account balance.
3   The year's charges for depreciation (found in that profit and loss account).

This has been done under the heading 'Issued Capital and Reserves' in

Exhibit 41

SOURCE AND APPLICATION OF FUNDS

Statement for the year ended ...

	£000	£000
SOURCES OF FUNDS		
Issued Capital and Reserves:		
Share capital		140
Reserves	285	
Add Depreciation	47	332
Net increase in shareholders' funds		472
Loan capital		50
Current Liabilities:		
Increases in		
Creditors and accrued expenses	95	
Taxation due	20	
Bills payable	45	
	160	
Less Decrease in bank overdraft	75	85
NET SUPPLY OF FUNDS		£607
APPLICATIONS OF FUNDS		
Fixed Assets:		
Net increase in fixed assets	160	
Add Depreciation in the year	47	207
Cost of control of subsidiary		35
Investments		7
Current Assets:		
Increases in		
Stocks	118	
Debtors	159	
Bank and cash	41	318
Capital expenses		40
NET APPLICATIONS OF FUNDS		£607

Exhibit 41. Here the year 2 cash flow is shown to be £332,000, and in the complete statement the cash flow from operations forms part of the total inflow of shareholders' funds. (The reader must note that, where a dividend had been paid or proposed during the year, a net cash flow total derived in the above way would be the post-tax, post-dividend net cash flow). This total proprietorial financing of the year's inflow of funds is £472,000, i.e. approximately 78 per cent of the total £607,000.

Now the reader has been warned that a published consolidated balance sheet (such as that from which the Funds Flow Statement has been derived) will not normally give the whole details of a year's changes in the corporate asset/liability status. To get a more complete picture of the firm's funds flow, one has to examine:

1   The notes accompanying the balance sheet.
2   The parent company's balance sheet.

In this instance the parent company's balance sheet is shown in Exhibit 17. A study of this exhibit will reveal that certain of the fixed assets were revalued: their book worth was increased by £100,000, as was the reserves section of the total shareholders' interest. Clearly, a revaluation reserve does not involve any transfer of funds. It is merely a book entry which gives recognition to a specific increase in the firm's asset wealth and consequently in the worth of the shareholders' investment. It has to be admitted therefore that the increase in reserves of £285,000 which is shown in Exhibit 41 should really be £185,000 only when we are reporting *fund* flows. Similarly the increase in shareholders' fund would then be £372,000 i.e. approximately 73 per cent of the now revised total of £507,000.

Yet another aspect of the parent company's financing strategy is revealed by an examination of its own balance sheet: £50,000 of preference shares were redeemed during the year. If we wished to give a full statement of the sources of funds for the Growing Group in year 2, then we should present the Issued Capital and Reserves items thus:

	£000	£000
Ordinary share capital		190
Reserves	185	
Add Depreciation	47	232
Increase in equity funds		422
Less Preference shares redeemed		50
Net increase in shareholders' funds		£372

These explanations should not discourage the reader from compiling corporate Funds Flow Statements. Exhibit 41 is still an acceptable picture of the overall changes in corporate wealth for the year in question. The more explicit data about the variation in proprietorial financing — given above — merely demonstrates how the several items of information which are given in the published accounts booklets, can be used. The important point about the revised figures, which should not be overlooked, is that they reveal a critical swing in the corporate policy for long term financing. The directing management appear to have decided on a move from preference share finance to loan stock finance. It would be of interest to see whether this policy was being pursued, when the next balance sheet of the Growing Group was published.

Working capital flow

Two further demonstrations of funds flow layout will now be examined. The first example (Exhibit 42) is drawn to reveal the causes of changes in working capital during the past year. Here the information given in Exhibits 40 and 41 has been slightly rearranged to accomplish this end. Furthermore the exhibit incorporates the more detailed data about changes in shareholders' funds, and the actual *expenditure* on fixed assets.

The impact upon the Growing Group's bank and cash balances can also be presented by a funds flow statement. Exhibit 43 shows this aspect of the firm's progress.

Corporate development

Exhibits 40 to 43 will have enabled the reader to see how the growth in book worth of the Growing Group's assets has been achieved. Here it is of importance to identify

1   The extent to which the increase in corporate asset wealth has been financed by the receipt of long-term capital money — compared with the amount financed by an internally generated cash flow.

2   The extent to which the working capital has increased in comparison with the modest increase in fixed assets.

Item 2 is relevant to the Growing Group's credit-worthiness. The financial advisers of the Group appear to be building a sound liquidity state in readiness for an expansion in the corporate operations. Where fixed asset and/or sales expansion occurs at the expense of a satisfactory working capital, then overtrading may lead to insolvency and the ultimate liquidation of the company.

Reference has been made on page 98 to the parent company's changing financial structure, and the fact that subsequent balance sheets and funds flow statements would reveal whether this development was being pursued, whether the group intended to move towards a higher level of gearing or not. By a continuance of this particular study, it might be possible to forecast the next share issue, or rights issue, or when an issue of loan stock was imminent. On the other

Exhibit 42

WORKING CAPITAL FLOW

Statement for the year ended ...

	£000	£000	£000
Working capital at 1 January			32
SOURCES OF FUNDS			
Ordinary share capital		190	
Reserves	185		
Add Depreciation	47	232	
Increase in equity funds		422	
Less Preference shares redeemed		50	
Net increase in shareholders' funds		372	
Loan capital		50	
Net supply of long-term funds			422
			454
APPLICATIONS OF FUNDS			
Fixed Assets:			
Net expenditure on fixed assets	60		
Add Depreciation in year	47	107	
Cost of control of subsidiary		35	
Investments		7	
Capital expenses		40	
Net expenditure on long-term items			189
Working capital as at 31 December			£265

hand increases in the firm's manufacturing capacity or modernisations of its existing plant will be brought into prominence by funds flow statements. When these changes are compared with sources of new funds, then the analyst can find out who is financing the growth in the corporate fixed assets. One would hope that growths in productive capacity were not being financed by short-term creditors. Long-term assets should be bought out of (a) long-term funds brought into the company and (b) net cash flows generated by trading operations. It has to be remembered however that some part at least of the internally generated cash flow will be needed to finance working capital growths.

The above comments have been made to interest the reader in the purpose and value of funds flow statements. These statements are not merely interesting arithmetical exercises — they are valuable means of interpreting company progress.

Exhibit 43

FUNDS FLOW

Statement for the year ended ...

	£000	£000
Cash in hand at 1 January	4	
Cash overdrawn at 1 January	(75)	(71)
SOURCES OF FUNDS		
Net increase in shareholders' funds	372	
Loan capital	50	
Net increases in current liabilities other than bank and cash	160	582
		511
APPLICATIONS OF FUNDS		
Net expenditure on fixed assets	107	
Cost of control of subsidiary	35	
Investments	7	
Net increases in current assets other than bank and cash	277	
Capital expenses	40	466
Total of cash and bank balances at 31 December		£45

The profit and loss accounts of the Courtaulds and Tesco groups are given in Exhibits 44 and 45 so that the reader can apply the knowledge which he has gained thus far, in practical cash flow calculation and analysis. No inter-company comparisons of profit performance, or of cost/income relationships are intended. Indeed such comparisons would be unrealistic because the two companies operate in entirely different fields.

Nevertheless in appraising the corporate cash flows generated by trading operations we shall need to eliminate, from both profit and loss accounts, those entries which represent

1   Non-cash flows, e.g. depreciation.
2   Non-company items, e.g. minority interests — share of profits of associated companies.
3   Non-trading items, e.g. realisation profits — interest receivable and payable.

The transactions under 2 are to be eliminated because our object is to determine the cash flows resulting from the groups' direct control and operation of their *own* corporate trading assets. In this matter we shall not be concerned with that part of the total trading profits which

1   Belong to the minority shareholders of subsidiary companies.
2   Arise from a group's interests in other associated companies.

So far as the non-trading items are concerned any capital profits, derived from the disposal of fixed assets and investments, must clearly be deducted. These transactions do not describe the outcomes of normal revenue trading. Such capital amounts will vary from year to year and will have little or no relationship with the level of trading. But it is the *trading* cash flow which is being studied here. Other non-trading items such as interest receivable and payable will normally be regarded in the same light. However Tesco's interest income appears to be the result of efficient management of the surplus cash resources (see the current assets in the balance sheet on pages 54 — 5). Similarly Courtauld's investment income includes interests receivable from short-term deposits — again an efficient use of surplus cash (this data is also given in the notes supporting the account). Therefore the cash flow statements in Exhibits 46 and 47 do not show these particular interest receivables to be deducted in arriving at the final cash flow totals.

If the information given in the published accounts booklets of these two firms is scrutinised, then we find that the commitments of the two groups for future capital expenditures — as at the end of each of the three years was as shown in Exhibits 48 and 49.

Exhibit 44

PUBLISHED GROUP PROFIT AND LOSS ACCOUNTS -
COURTAULDS LIMITED

Details	1974		1973		1972	
	£000	£000	£000	£000	£000	£000
Sales		956776		777129		681488
Trading profits		162380		115916		92510
Deduct:						
Depreciation	41896		37045		34994	
Auditors' fees and expenses	710		628		592	
Interest payable	24761		20163		19039	
Hire of plant & equipment	2134	69501	1924	59760	1641	56266
		92879		56156		36244
Add:						
Interest receivable*	18315		6959		4442	
Realisation profits	924		2724		2797	
Associated companies	4152	23391	2325	12008	2084	9323
Profits before tax		116270		68164		45567
Deduct: Taxation		26930		12301		5728
Profits after tax		89340		55863		39839
Deduct: Minority interests		5624		3710		3167
Attributable to shareholders		£83716		£52153		£36672

*Includes dividends from quoted and unquoted investments:
1974 - £974; 1973 - £618; 1972 - £611

Exhibit 45

PUBLISHED GROUP PROFIT AND LOSS ACCOUNTS - TESCO

Details	1974		1973		1972	
	£000	£000	£000	£000	£000	£000
Sales		423032		359013		299701
Trading profits		27461		25328		20637
Deduct:						
Depreciation	5054		4490		4402	
Auditors' fees and expenses	37		33		29	
Interest payable	34	5125	36	4559	40	4471
		22336		20769		16166
Add:						
Interest and dividends receivable.		2202		958		376
Profits before tax		24538		21727		16542
Deduct: Taxation		12808		9007		6735
Profits after tax attributable to shareholders		£11730		£12720		£9807

Exhibit 46

CASH FLOWS GENERATED BY TRADING OPERATIONS - COURTAULDS

Details	1974		1973		1972	
	£000	£000	£000	£000	£000	£000
Post-tax profits (see Exhibit 44)		89340		55863		39839
Add:						
Depreciation in year	41896		37045		34994	
Interest payable	24761		20163		19039	
Tax relating to trading profit of associated companies	1005	67662	560	57768	599	54632
		157002		113631		94471
Less:						
Realisation profits (surpluses on disposal of fixed assets)	924		2724		2797	
Share of pre-tax trading profits of associated companies	4152		2325		2084	
Investment income	974		618		611	
Profits attributable to minority interests	5264	11314	3710	9377	3167	8659
Operating cash flows		£145688		£104254		£85812

When these annual cash flow amounts are compared with the relevant yearly forecasts for additional capital expenditures, we shall see whether either of the two firms could finance their developments from internally generated cash flows. In this connection, however, we must remember that the forecast capital expenditure figures do not necessarily mean that such expenditure sums WILL be incurred in the succeeding year. It is clear from this that both groups have, during the past three years, moved from a state where they could pay for their new investments in capital assets from internally generated funds to a state where they would need additional finance in order to complete the whole of the works envisaged. With regard to Tesco, the summation of the three years' figures shows that a sufficient internal cash flow has been generated to meet the expected capital expenditures of those three years. Furthermore it is unlikely that working capital needs will grow in this group and therefore will not absorb any — or much — of the cash flows. On the other hand Courtauld's trading cash flows are insufficient to cover the forecast capital expenditures. Also we have seen that the group's investments in working capital have grown by over £90m between 1972 and 1974, and we might expect this growth to continue especially during the inflation era. Thus we can see further evidence of the need for the group's increases in Loan Capital — referred to on pages 72/3. But it must be remembered that both groups have other non-trading cash flows: it must also be remembered that, in addition to any future increases in working capital requirements, the payments of dividends to shareholders and interest to loan stockholders will absorb some of

Exhibit 47

CASH FLOWS GENERATED BY TRADING OPERATIONS - TESCO

Details	1974		1973		1972	
	£000	£000	£000	£000	£000	£000
Post-tax profits		11730		12720		9807
Add:						
Depreciation in year	5054		4490		4402	
Interest payable	34	5088	36	4526	40	4442
Operating cash flows		£16818		£17246		£14249

the operating cash flows. The vital lesson for the reader to learn is
that the simple cash flow calculation, shown on the previous page,
has to be appraised against the various uses to which cash flows may
be applied such as

New capital investment

Additional working capital

Dividend and interest payments

Therefore it is emphasised again that a positive cash flow sum does
not portend a similar increase in the firm's cash at bank. With
increases in the rate of inflation, where restraint on the selling prices
of the firm's goods is enforced, then operating cash flows may be

Exhibit 48

Details	1974 £000	1973 £000	1972 £000
Courtaulds			
Uncompleted contracts	90400	31600	7300
Authorised but not yet contracted	71800	87200	14500
Totals	£162200	£118800	£21800
Tesco			
Uncompleted contracts	10388	10100	6919
Authorised but not yet contracted	10102	6902	1451
Totals	£20490	£17002	£8370

Exhibit 49

	1974 £000	1973 £000	1972 £000
Courtaulds			
Forecast capital expenditure	162200	118800	21800
Cash flows	145688	104254	85812
	£(16512)	£(14546)	£64012
Tesco			
Forecast capital expenditure	20490	17002	8370
Cash flows	16818	17246	14249
	£(3672)	£244	£5879

insufficient to finance a merely static level of business: rising costs will so impact upon working capital requirements (for stock and debtors) that externally raised money will be needed to enable a business to maintain its existing rate of operations.

Further reading

R.H. Parker and G.C. Harcourt (Editors), *Readings in the concept and measurement of income,* Cambridge University Press (1969).

L.E. Rockley, *The non-accountant's guide to finance,* Business Books (1972).

P.E. Fertig, D.F. Istvan and H.J. Mottice, *Using accounting information: an introduction,* Harcourt Brace (Second edition, 1971). (See especially Parts 3 and 4).

R.K. Jaedicke and R.T. Sprouse, *Accounting flows: income, funds and cash,* Prentice Hall (1965). See especially Chapters V - VII.

W. Beranek, *Working capital management,* Wadsworth (1966).

'Where have all the profits gone,' *The Accountant,* pp 697-8 (27 May 1971).

'Funds flow statements: how and why', *Accountancy,* pp 644-9 (September 1970).

Perry Mason, *Cash flow analysis and the fund statement,* research study by Association of Certified Public Accountants, USA.

Profitability and Market Worth | *4*

Introduction

The work of the previous chapters has been concerned with the construction of balance sheets, and conclusions which may be drawn from data which normally appear in such statements. Our balance sheets have yielded information on financial structure, asset strength, liquidity and credit worthiness. The reader has furthermore been able to trace the impact of a year's trading upon these various aspects of the corporate whole. Each of the analyses so far studied would be an integral part of a complete appraisal of any company's standing in business affairs.

The anatomy of return on capital employed

By using relevant data from the profit and loss accounts, outlined in Chapter 3, we can evaluate corporate profitability and market worth.

Now profitability and market worth are concerned with more than just an absolute amount of profit, more than just the book value of a firm's possessions. Profitability and market worth connote some comparisons of net income earned with the invested cost of getting that income. Inevitably one turns to the ratio of return on capital employed (ROC) in order to establish some measure of profit earning ability. This ratio is expressed by the formula

$$\text{ROC} = \frac{\text{Return (net income earned)}}{\text{Capital employed}} \times 100$$

Calculations of profitability percentages for each of the various definitions of capital employed* give useful measures of corporate performance for the different groups of investors and traders who study the affairs of commercial and industrial firms. Yet the use of ROC as an effective measure of profit earning ability is severely criticised. These criticisms stem mainly from the use of unrealistic asset book values within the quantum of the term 'capital employed'. Such asset book values — as are revealed in most balance sheets — result from their acquisition costs which were incurred some years ago. Furthermore these cost-based book values are reduced year after year by each year's depreciation charges, despite the fact that the assets' value in use may be rising. If a particular asset is retained long enough, the accumulated total of annual depreciation charges may well bring its balance sheet (book) value to nil, even though the asset continues to make an acceptable contribution to corporate productivity. To meet this problem some reassessment of the book value of such an asset becomes necessary and future depreciation charges levied in yearly profit and loss accounts should then be based upon the re-assessed sum.

Nevertheless, so long as company final accounts reflect the use of historic acquisition costs, then the data recorded in profit and loss accounts and balance sheets will be based upon factual monetary transactions. The 'factual monetary transactions' quality of historic reporting has always been regarded as a principal advantage of that concept. Historic cost accounting limits the impact which subjective opinion or judgement can have upon the data contained in the final accounts+. Thus it affects the figures used in the ROC calculations.

*The concepts of total capital employed, capital invested and shareholders' capital are explained in Chapter 2, pages 61 — 64.

+Calculations of annual depreciation charges will remain a product of opinion, rather than the result of a scientific measurement of observed changes in the worths of corporate assets.

But when the purchasing power of the monetary unit suffers marked changes over the years, then its value as a comparative measuring rod is considerably weakened. This means that when a current profit is quoted as a percentage of past capital investment expressed in historic cost terms, then the consequent ROC percentage cannot represent a realistic appraisal of business performance. It will not bring the economic worth of the profit into comparison with the *up to date* invested cost of earning it. In an attempt to meet this deficiency some companies revalue some of their assets so as to bring them into line with purchasing power values existing at the date of the revaluation. However, when such piecemeal adjustments are introduced to deal with the problems of unstable money values, they serve only to confuse the issue. A complete system of accounting for changes in the purchasing power of money must be recommended, for more realistic data bases will give rise to more realistic percentage ratings for the appraisal of business activities. This topic forms the subject matter of Chapter 5.

But the fact remains that ROC is our commonly used measure of *over-all* business performance. The ratio purports to show, in a single percentage figure, the efficiency and profitability of the various sectors of the corporate whole. When we recognise that business firms have diverse departments such as production, marketing, selling, finance, transport, research and development etc., we realise that the business analyst will need other supporting criteria to effect a complete evaluation of a firm's performance. We cannot expect a single ROC percentage rate to tell the full story. Additional appraisal criteria could include

1   Output per man hour or per machine hour
2   Output as a multiple of fixed assets or of working capital
3   Sales per employee
4   Profits per employee
5   Vehicle running costs per mile or per unit of goods conveyed.

Here it is pointed out that the ROC index can itself be analysed in order to trace many of the other factors which contribute to a particular percentage rating. Exhibit 50 shows how the single ratio is affected by various aspects of a firm's operations and structure. When these other cost/income relationships are presented in ratio form, the analyst will be able to identify some of the reasons why the corporate ROC stands at say 10 per cent, and how that rating could be improved. At least it will bring into prominence those areas of corporate activity to which management's remedial action should be directed.

Exhibit 50

PERFORMANCE EVALUATION RATIO ANALYSIS

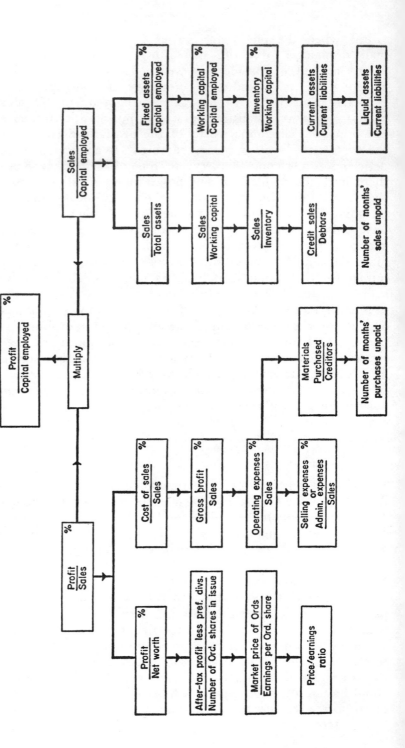

The reader should note the first two constituents of the ROC ratio,
namely
1   The rate of profit generated by Sales.
2   The rate at which sales are generated by using corporate assets.

These prime constituents of ROC can be expressed by the equation

$$\frac{\text{Return x 100}}{\text{Capital employed}} = \frac{\text{Return x 100}}{\text{Sales}} \times \frac{\text{Sales}}{\text{Capital employed}}$$

The right-hand side of the above equation should not be dismissed as being merely a longer way of describing ROC. Additional vital information is given. For example an ROC of 10 per cent could result from either:

1   A 10 per cent profit on sales X 1, i.e. the rate at which sales are generated or £1 of sales for every £1 worth of capital employed.
2   A 5 per cent profit on sales X 2
3   A 4 per cent profit on sales X 2.5

So if the profit rate on sales in (1) above could be accompanied by the sales generation rate in (3) above, the average over-all ROC for the firm would be 10 per cent X 2.5 = 25 per cent.

The simple example given above indicates how an improved company profitability may be sought. At the same time Exhibit 50 will guide the corporate planner to other areas of the firm's business where the need for improved performances may be revealed by ratio analysis. However there is a limit to our ability to secure an increased ROC, merely by improving *one* ratio. To clarify this point, the Exhibit 51 has been prepared to show the profiles of a 5 per cent and a 10 per cent return on capital employed. This exhibit shows that with an ROC of 5 per cent and a net return on sales of 5 per cent, the rate of turnover of capital employed would have to be 1, i.e. once per year. If it was desired to secure an ROC of 10 per cent whilst maintaining the return on sales at 5 per cent, then the rate of turnover of capital employed would have to rise to 2. BUT if we had a rate of turnover of capital employed of only 0.1, then if we still required a 10 per cent ROC, the return on sales would have to be 100 per cent! A 100 per cent return on sales would mean that there were *no costs* of sales, which would be patently unrealistic. Obviously any improvement in corporate ROC must be a function of more than one facet of the firm's operations. In the above example the rate of turnover of capital employed would have to be increased also.

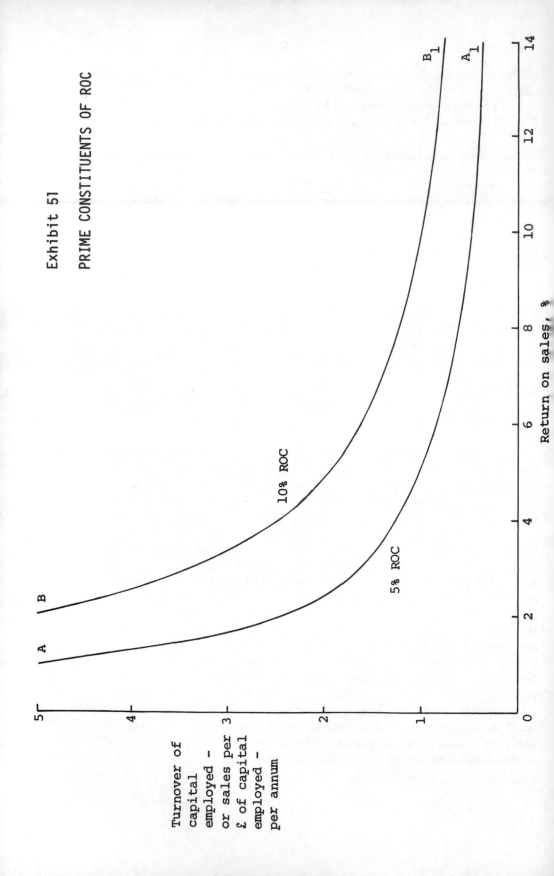

Exhibit 51

PRIME CONSTITUENTS OF ROC

A study can now be made of the Growing Group's progress in year 2 and the results of that year can be compared with those of year 1. Exhibit 52 describes the three interpretations of capital employed and explains the appropriate return concept to be used with each separate definition. The figures quoted have been taken from the Growing Group's balance sheets given on page 51 and the profit and loss accounts on page 90. The exhibit goes on to define the ratios of Return on Sales and of Turnover of Capital Employed: each of these performance indices have been calculated for the reader's guidance. In studying Exhibit 52 the reader must note that ratios 4 and 5 in the table have been worked out by reference to the definitions of return and capital employed which are specified in ratio 2 — the return on long-term investment.

Throughout the table the immediate aims which each ratio sets out to meet have been quoted: a statement is also given of those groups of people who are likely to be interested in the information thus being revealed. If we now use the ROC equation given on page 113 and transfer data from Exhibit 52 the trend of results is shown to be

Year 1 : $11.4\% = 2.53\% \times 4.52$
Year 2 : $13.2\% = 3.2\% \times 4.14$

From these ratios we can see that
1   For every £1's worth of sales the amount of profit generated in year 1 was 2.53p : in year 2, this had risen to 3.2p per £ of sales.
2   For every £1's worth of capital employed the amount of sales generated in year 1 was £4.52 : in year 2, this was slightly lower at £4.14 per £ of capital employed.
The combination of the two prime influences upon ROC reveals an overall profit ability rating which rises from 11.4 per cent in year 1 to 13.2 per cent in year 2 : a year of steady, but not startling, improvement.

From this point on, our analysis of any firm's profitability rating will be conditioned by the size and type of the business being studied. Exhibit 50 gives a picture of some of the stages in a programme of corporate appraisal. Special situations will demand other actions however. Thus in the present environment of ever-rising labour costs, managers need to pay greater attention to the impact of this factor upon the firm's power to generate profit.

To demonstrate the kind of ratios we can use in this situation, we will assume that the size of the Growing Group's labour force, and its related annual wages bill for the two years, were as follows:

Exhibit 52

ANALYSIS OF RETURN ON CAPITAL EMPLOYED

No.	Ratio	Interested parties	Aims of ratio	Capital employed (book value) Year 1 £000	Year 2 £000	Return Year 1 £000	Year 2 £000	Per cent rating Year 1 %	Year 2 %
1	*Return on Total Capital Employed:* includes only tangible assets used in the business' trading operations; investments outside the business are excluded. The return describes profit before tax and interest and excludes income from investments.	Management	To show how well the firm is performing in terms of rate of profit earned by its normal trading activities	657	1135	38	96	5.8	8.5
2	*Return on Capital Invested:* includes only tangible assets used in the business' trading operations less current liabilities: investments outside the business are also excluded. The return describes profit before tax and interest and excludes income from investments	Long-term investors and lenders of money to the company. Other companies may be interested in the profitability of the Growing Group.	Enables investors and lenders to judge the worthwhileness and soundness of their investment. Also enables inter-firm comparisons.	332	725	38	96	11.4	13.2

Ratio	Used by	Purpose						
Return on Shareholders' Funds: describes the return to the *Ordinary* shareholders' total funds; it therefore refers to the Total Shareholders' Interest *less* any Preference shares in issue. The return refers to *all* profits after tax *less* Preference dividends.	Existing Ordinary shareholders of the company and potential buyers of the firm's shares.	Shows the worth of investing in the company's Ordinary shares; may be compared with the returns obtained from investing in other companies.	250	685	14	62	5.6	9.1
Return on Sales: describes profit before interest and before tax but excluding investment income – expressed as a percentage of sales	Management	To show the operational efficiency of company in its manufacturing, warehousing, management, selling and distribution of its products	Sales 1500	Sales 3000	38	96	2.53	3.2
Turnover of Capital Employed: describes the rate at which the business generates sales by the use of its operating capital employed	Management	To show how well the firm is organised in its production operations. It shows how effectively the firm uses its assets to produce sales.	C.E. 332	C.E. 725	Sales 1500	Sales 3000	Times 4.52	Times 4.14

	Year 1	Year 2
Number of employees	150	225
Total wage and salary costs	£300,000	£400,000

The relevant turnover and trading profit for each of the two years is given in Exhibit 38 as

	Year 1 £	Year 2 £
Turnover	1,500,000	3,000,000
Pre-tax trading profit	38,000	96,000

Comparison of the above two groups of data enables us to compile the following ratios

	Year 1 £	Year 2 £
Sales per employee	10,000	13,333
Profits per employee	253.3	426.6
Sales per £ of wage and salary costs	5	7.5
Profits per £ of wage and salary cost	0.127	0.24

When appropriate input/output data are analysed in this way, we can establish control indices which will reveal those areas of weakness or of strength in the achievement of corporate profitability. Comparative ratio analysis demands that our control indices be matched with similar data derived from the reports and accounts of other companies, and from other periods in the life of the same firm. Meaningful comparisons with the performances of other firms would have to be confined to firms of

1   A similar size, engaged in a similar trade, and, preferably,
2   A similar age.

But some worthwhile guide-lines may be achieved by going outside these parameters so long as the analyst recognises the different circumstances which will exist and which may affect the relative performances.

Business profitability and liquidity can be seriously impaired by the rising costs of holding stocks and of financing debtors. The management of working capital involves stock control, the operation of maximum and minimum stock holding and re-ordering quantities, policies of credit control and the effective use of cash flow to secure, for example, discounts for prompt payment of supplier's invoices. We can again establish control indices which can be of considerable importance for maintaining a good liquidity status. The relationship of creditors to stocks will reveal whether supply prices are rising faster than our ability to convert the goods into profitable sales — assuming that the level of business remains constant. (It may also be an indication that the firm does not pay its creditors so promptly as previously.) Appropriate information from the balance sheets of the Growing Group (page 51) is used in the calculations below:

	Year 1	Year 2
$\dfrac{\text{Creditors} \times 100}{\text{Stock}} =$	$\dfrac{190,000 \times 100}{252,000}$	$\dfrac{285,000 \times 100}{370,000}$

Therefore creditors as percentage of stock

	Year 1	Year 2
=	75.4	77

It is stressed that the percentage relationship will vary with different companies. The nature of the business, the length of time necessary to convert raw material into a saleable commodity are material factors to take into account. Nevertheless one would not wish to see the percentage rating to continue rising above 80 per cent. (In this example creditors and accrued expenses have been compared with all kinds of stock, as this is the data normally shown in published accounts. For more precise calculations for internal management, one would compare *trade* creditors with *raw material* stocks. A more detailed analysis of stock turnover rates is given in *The Non-accountant's guide to finance* (L. E. Rockley, Business Books, pp. 73-4).

With high interest charges for normal bank overdrafts, and even higher rates to be levied when the approved overdraft limit is exceeded it becomes imperative to regulate the period (and amount) of credit given to the customers. After all when the value of money is declining, a debt due to the firm soon begins to decrease in real value, when receipt of the money is unreasonably delayed. An appropriate control ratio is exemplified below. The data used relates to the

Growing Group and they show that when the average daily credit sales (annual credit sales divided by 365) are divided into the balance sheet sum of debtors, the resultant figure represents the average number of days credit given by the company to its customers:

	Year 1	Year 2
$\dfrac{\text{Debtors at year end}}{\text{Average daily sales}} =$	$\dfrac{101,000}{1,500,000 \div 365}$	$\dfrac{260,000}{3,000,000 \div 365}$
$=$	$\dfrac{101,000 \times 365}{1,500,000}$	$\dfrac{260,000 \times 365}{3,000,000}$
$=$	24.6 days	31.6 days

The shrewd manager will realise that if he decides to allow his customers 28 days in which to settle their accounts, AND if he knows the average daily rate of his credit sales to be — say about £6,000, then he can expect his total debtors to approximate to £168,000. Whilst full credit control demands more than this simple calculation, it does however give a broad rule-of-thumb appraisal of the working capital requirements which credit giving entails.

The reader should now pursue his analyses of corporate performance by examining the chain of ratios shown in Exhibit 50. In particular, control indices should be tested and established in order to demonstrate the major influences upon corporate/sales profitability of

1   Operating expenses: each major group of expense should be quoted as a percentage of the related sales values and the percentage factor should be under monthly observation.
2   The amount of capital invested in fixed assets and in working capital: here the relevant comparisons will be sales per £ of fixed assets and sales per £ of working capital.

Courtaulds and Tesco

A similar exercise can be completed for our two public companies — Courtaulds and Tesco. A study of their balance sheets (pages 53 and 55) will show their long-term capital invested in each of the past three years to be as given in Exhibit 53. Furthermore the company profit and loss accounts reproduced on pages 103-4 enables us to compute appropriate pre-tax trading profits. Exhibit 54 presents the data.

The reader should note that, in order to calculate appropriate profit amounts which can be attributed to the particular mix of operating assets employed, we have not

1 Continued the previous deduction for interest on borrowed money.
2 Included any income which arose from transactions other than normal group trading activities.
3 Deducted the amounts received for interest on money lent by the firms.

With regard to item 3 these amounts have been retained in the 'trading return on capital invested' because the income results from management's efficient use of (temporary) surplus cash resources. The interest income does not arise from a long term *investment* in the debentures of other companies.

Therefore if we use these data of capital invested and of the trading return, together with the annual sales figures given in Exhibit 44 we can complete ROC equations for the past three years. The resultant ratios are tabulated in Exhibit 55.

Exhibit 53

CAPITAL INVESTED TOTALS

	1974 £000	1973 £000	1972 £000
Courtaulds Limited			
Fixed assets	354161	300377	290097
Current assets	605477	471830	385686
	959638	772207	675783
Less Current liabilities	287692	179325	159865
CAPITAL INVESTED	£671946	£592882	£515918
Tesco Limited			
Fixed assets	67329	58082	53925
Current assets	65907	50573	32093
	133236	108655	86018
Less Current liabilities	68546	50248	37060
CAPITAL INVESTED	£64690	£58407	£48958

Exhibit 54

PRE-TAX TRADING PROFITS

Courtaulds Limited

Details	1974 £000	£000	1973 £000	£000	1972 £000	£000
Profits before tax		116270		68164		45567
Add Interest amounts previously deducted from above profits		24761		20163		19039
		141031		88327		64606
Less Amounts previously included in the above profits for:						
(a) income from quoted and unquoted investments	974		618		611	
(b) capital profits	924		2724		2797	
(c) share of profits of associated companies	4152	6050	2325	5667	2084	5492
Trading return on capital invested		£134981		£82660		£59114

Tesco Limited

Details	1974 £000	1973 £000	1972 £000
Profits before tax	24538	21727	16542
Add Interest amounts previously deducted from the above profits	34	36	40
Trading return on capital invested	£24572	£21763	£16582

Exhibit 55

PERFORMANCE EVALUATION

Details	COURTAULDS LIMITED			TESCO LIMITED		
	Return on capital invested	Return on sales	Sales per £ of capital invested	Return on capital invested	Return on sales	Sales per £ of capital invested
1974	$\frac{134981}{671946} \times 100$ = 20.09%	$\frac{134981}{956776} \times 100$ = 14.11%	$\frac{956776}{671946}$ = £1.42	$\frac{24572}{64690} \times 100$ = 37.98%	$\frac{24572}{423032} \times 100$ = 5.81%	$\frac{423032}{64690}$ = £6.54
1973	$\frac{82660}{592882} \times 100$ = 13.94%	$\frac{82660}{777129} \times 100$ = 10.64%	$\frac{777129}{592882}$ = £1.31	$\frac{21763}{58407} \times 100$ = 37.26%	$\frac{21763}{359013} \times 100$ = 6.06%	$\frac{359013}{58407}$ = £6.15
1972	$\frac{59114}{515918} \times 100$ = 11.46%	$\frac{59114}{681488} \times 100$ = 8.67%	$\frac{681488}{515918}$ = £1.32	$\frac{16582}{48958} \times 100$ = 33.87%	$\frac{16582}{299701} \times 100$ = 5.53%	$\frac{299701}{48958}$ = £6.12

Careful studies of the published accounts booklets of the UK companies will reward the analyst. For example, *The Companies Act, 1967,* at section 18 requires the following to be reported:

1   The average number of persons employed in each week.
2   Their aggregate remuneration for the year.

We are therefore able to calculate comparative control ratios such as those demonstrated in the examination of the Growing Group's progress. Exhibit 56 (right) exemplifies the use of data which are generally available in the published accounts booklets issued by all UK companies: the exhibit does not propose comparisons between the companies involved because these firms operate in different trading areas.

We can extend our analysis to embrace working capital management by producing credit control and stock turnover ratios etc. The information is there to use but we have to remember that our conclusions will be based upon figures derived from the firm's PAST activities. Trends of historical data may be useful in that they may give indications of potential progress in the future. Nevertheless it is facts about the current and future expected trading returns which are more relevant, and a study of the Directors' Report (a copy of which must be sent with the accounts to all members of the company) may be of help here.

Thus, we would obtain a better picture of the profitability prospects for the (near) future if we could secure information from any firm about

1   The size of the current order book.
2   The stability of the work force.
3   Its management succession plans.
4   The efficiency state of the business assets.
5   The *current* liquidity state of the firm.

Earnings per share and market worth

Indications of current opinion about the trading prospects of UK companies can be obtained by studying the movements in Stock Exchange prices for their shares. Such information is not wholly reliable however: it reflects the impacts of events which may be totally unconnected with the company concerned. The Stock Market is quick to react unfavourably to such matters as poor returns from one of the industrial giants, balance of payments crises, or even the prospects of a General Election! Stock Exchange share price movements merely represent the combined views of the buyers and sellers of industrial and commercial shares.

Exhibit 56

SELECTED COMPANIES – PERFORMANCE AND CREDIT RATIOS

Company	YEAR	Pre-tax return on		Sales as a multiple of		Sales per employee	Pre-tax profits	Sales per £ wages	Pre-tax profits per £ wages	Current ratio	Liquid ratio
		Capital employed %	Sales %	Capital employed £	Working capital £	£	£	£	£		
TESCO LIMITED	1974	37.98	5.81	6.54	–	10511	610.6	11.32	0.66	0.96	0.26
	1973	37.26	6.06	6.15	1105	10478	635.2	12.65	0.77	1.0	0.39
	1972	33.87	5.53	6.12	–	9349	517.3	12.41	0.69	0.87	0.11
COURTAULDS LIMITED	1974	20.09	14.11	1.42	3.01	7686	1084.4	4.96	0.70	2.1	1.33
	1973	13.94	10.64	1.31	2.65	6265	666.4	4.63	0.49	2.6	1.5
	1972	11.46	8.67	1.32	3.01	5322	461.7	4.47	0.39	2.4	1.3
BOOKER AND McCONNEL LIMITED	1973	19.49	5.45	3.58	21.96	15403	839.5	12.81	0.698	1.16	0.53
	1972	18.35	5.85	3.13	15.55	15937	932.3	13.64	0.798	1.28	0.55
	1971	16.82	6.10	2.75	14.98					1.25	0.55
MARKS AND SPENCER LIMITED	1974	30.47	12.17	2.5	–	14822	1803.9	14.02	1.71	0.88	0.42
	1973	34.8	13.3	2.62	46.68	14834	1973.7	14.98	1.99	1.16	0.76
	1972	31.08	12.29	2.53	430.31	13022	1601.5	14.89	1.83	1.02	0.55

If we return to the Growing Group's profit and loss account and calculate the amount of post tax profits belonging to the ordinary shareholders, we should be able to come to some conclusions about the worth of these shares.

Exhibit 57 tells us that the ordinary shareholder has earned a better return in year 2 than he had in year 1. This could point to the possibility of a higher price for these shares in year 2 than was obtained in year 1. But in the context of a falling market, one would hope that any tendency towards a fall in price of the Growing Group's ordinary shares would be moderated by the rising EPS figures.

Each day the financial press publishes an index which measures the effect of price, dividend, etc., movements of a representative sample of quoted ordinary shares. A feature of this published information is the price earnings ratio (P/E ratio). Now an Ordinary share's P/E ratio is calculated by dividing its market price by the past or the expected EPS for that share.
Thus, if the

```
Market price of a share = £2.00
```

and the

```
EPS = 10p
```

then the

$$\text{P/E ratio} = £\frac{2.00}{0.10} = 20$$

Broadly the ratio of 20 indicates the number of years that an investor would have to wait for his EPS of 10p per year to enable him to recover his initial cost of investing £2.00 in buying such a share. More importantly a P/E ratio reflects the share market's evaluation of the expected future stream of earnings for the share involved. A high P/E ratio is an indication of the market's approval of that particular share which is accorded the high P/E rating. But it must be remembered that the business world is made up of many different sizes and types of firms which operate in widely differing industries. Also the risks attaching to business vary from trade to trade, and according to the size and age of the firm. Therefore the level of prices for ordinary shares will vary from firm to firm according to the appraisal by investors of the worthwhileness of investing in those varying trade/risk situations. Clearly there could not be a **single**

Exhibit 57   *127*

EARNINGS PER ORDINARY SHARE (EPS)

	Year 1 £000	Year 2 £000
Post-tax profits per PL account (page 91)	20	65
Less Preference dividend	6	3
Profits (or earnings) available for Ordinary shareholders	£14	£62
Number of Ordinary shares in issue (page 36)	60,000	250,000
Therefore earnings available for each Ordinary share	$= \pounds\dfrac{14,000}{60,000}$	$\pounds\dfrac{62,000}{250,000}$
	$= 23\text{p}$	25p

price level for equity investments throughout the whole of the business world. Neither is their a single 'good' P/E ratio for all of the firms quoted on the stock exchange. An evaluation of the investment opportunities presented by ordinary shares will be influenced by the potential investor's requirements. These requirements will be determined by the investor's attitudes to the expectations of
> High dividends
> Possible capital growth
> The stimulation of a calculated risk, or
> The security of the investment.

The market average*

The Financial Times/Actuaries Share Index published in the *Financial Times* each day reports, *inter alia,* an average P/E ratio derived from a sample of the companies quoted on the Stock Exchange. This averaged ratio is given for (a) the whole commercial and industrial

*The following pages deal with P/E ratios, earnings yield, dividend, dividend yield and dividend cover, and here the writer's object is to explain the concepts in simple form. Thus very precise definitions of earnings, dividend, dividend yield and cover will not be pursued at this point. The reader will be introduced to the imputation system of dividend taxation and its possible effects on the calculation of earnings per share etc. at a later stage.

field and (b) for each of the separate industrial, commercial and financial sectors.

A rough guide to the value of a company's ordinary shares can be obtained by multiplying the relevant EPS by the average sector P/E ratio revealed by the index. We can demonstrate the concept if we assume that the average P/E ratios for the ordinary shares of the Growing Group's industrial sector were 15 and 17 in years 1 and 2 respectively. If these ratios are matched with the appropriate EPS figures for the two years, then the Ordinary share valuations for the two years would be

$$\text{Year 1} : 23\text{p} \times 15 = £3.45$$
$$\text{Year 2} : 25\text{p} \times 17 = £4.25$$

The fact that a higher P/E ratio was experienced in year 2 than in year 1 can be explained. General confidence in the future outcomes of business activity may stimulate such an amount of trading on the stock exchange that a tendency will emerge for most share prices to rise. A rise in share price without a parallel rise in EPS — either actual or expected — must act to increase the P/E ratio. On the other hand, the publication of data showing increased EPS figures will more than likely stimulate an interest in that company's shares. Here both the market price *and* the P/E may rise. The extent to which the price of a share will continue to rise must depend upon the expectations which investors have of future increases in the EPS of the shares involved. So where a very high P/E ratio is found (say 40 or 50), such a high rating is an indication that the market has already discounted much of any future earnings increase which may accrue to the shares.

Earnings yield

Earnings yield describes the percentage relationship which an Ordinary share's earnings (EPS) bears to the market price of the share. In other words it specifies the profitability rate prospects from buying a share in the company because an investment in a company's Ordinary shares represents a purchase of a share in the future earnings of that company.

The earnings yield is expressed in percentage terms and therefore it enables comparisons to be made with the rewards obtainable from all other forms of investments, such as the building societies, unit trusts and other equity shares. The rate is calculated thus:

$$\frac{\text{Earnings per share} \times 100}{\text{Market price of the share}}$$

If we assume that the actual market prices of the ordinary shares in
the Growing Group were £3.45 and £4.25 in years 1 and 3, respectively, then the earnings yields for these two years* would be

$$\text{Year } 1 = \frac{0.23 \times 100}{3.45} = 6.7\%$$

$$\text{Year } 2 = \frac{0.25 \times 100}{4.25} = 5.9\%$$

Clearly the earnings yield concept is directly related to the P/E ratio,
for the same information is used in both types of calculation, e.g.

$$\text{P/E ratio} = \frac{\text{Market price per share}}{\text{Earnings per share}}$$

$$\text{Earnings yield} = \frac{\text{Earnings per share} \times 100}{\text{Market price per share}}$$

The relationship between the two ratios can be explained by saying
that the P/E ratio is the reciprocal of the earnings yield percentage.
Therefore if we use the earnings yield in the following way

Year 1 = 100/6.7

year 2 = 100/5.9

then the answers to the simple division sums will produce the P/E
ratios of 15 and 17. Again if we had taken these P/E ratios and worked
out their reciprocals, we would have arrived at the earnings yield,
thus

Year 1 = 100/15 = 6.7%

Year 2 = 100/17 = 5.9%

The reader should note that a rising P/E ratio will always be accompanied by a falling earnings yield. The reverse is also true. These
situations of rising P/E ratios and falling earnings yields indicate that
the ordinary shares to which they relate may be a worthwhile investment at the given market price. It would appear that the relevant
company is doing well and that its expected future profit earnings
capacity has been noted by investors on the Stock Market.

However it is emphasised that EPS — the vital feature in the above

*The statement 'earnings yields for these two years' refers to yields based upon
the *year-end figures* shown in the profit and loss accounts. *Throughout each of
the two years,* the yields would certainly have varied in response to market
fluctuations in the general level of share prices.

two ratios — is most frequently calculated from the profits after tax disclosed in the published profit and loss account. Now it is essential that the EPS statement should be based upon a level of profits which the company can be expected to maintain in the future. Furthermore, the analyst will need to examine the firm's methods of accounting for such items as

> Fixed asset depreciation
> Stock valuation
> Research and development costs

because they can have a material impact upon the amount of declared profits. Finally it has to be said that calculations of arithmetical ratios, estimated share prices etc. cannot take the place of personal judgement. At some stage in the analysis, the investigator's common sense and discrimination must be applied to an appraisal of those ratios he has calculated.

Dividend, dividend yield and dividend cover

The amount of the annual dividend received by a holder of Ordinary shares is an important factor in assessing the worth of the shares. It represents an income which the shareholder actually receives in cash. In this sense it is more of a direct benefit to the shareholder than any statement of earnings per share. But the payment of dividends depends in the main upon profitable trading, and therefore upon the post tax earnings of the company. Whilst the quantity of post tax earnings may be seen to set the upper limit of any annual dividends) in the last resource this is not so, for transfers from certain reserves to the profit and loss account can be made to enable a dividend to be declared) it is the amount of the dividends, plus the likelihood of their continuance, which stimulates so much attention from investors.

The dividend yield concept expresses the annual dividend per share as a percentage of the market price for the share. The formula for calculation of dividend yield is

```
Dividend per share x 100
 Market price per share
```

or

```
Total dividend paid x 100
   Market value of the
Ordinary shares in issue
```

The actual dividends are thus expressed as a percentage of the cost of buying that dividend, i.e. the market price of one Crdinary share.

Again this percentage can be compared with alternative methods of obtaining an income from saving or investment. In particular the dividend yield of a firm's Ordinary shares can be compared with that of the ordinary shares of other companies. Clearly total annual earnings are vital to a consideration of company worth, but where such earnings or any part thereof are not distributed to the shareholders as dividends, then their ultimate value to the shareholder must depend upon the efficiency with which corporate management uses those *retained* earnings.

The dividend yield calculations for years 1 and 2 of the Growing Group are shown below. In these examples the yield is calculated by reference to the total amount of dividends paid and the market capitalisation of the issued Ordinary shares. This market capitalisation is derived from the *number* of Ordinary shares in issue multiplied by the market price for one of those shares

$$\text{Year 1: } \frac{5,000 \times 100}{60,000 \times £3.45} = 2.41\%$$

$$\text{Year 2: } \frac{25,000 \times 100}{250,000 \times £4.25} = 2.35\%$$

When the rate of dividend was announced it would be quoted as a percentage of the nominal value of the shares. Therefore the dividend (NOT the dividend yield) was quoted 8.3 and 10 per cent for years 1 and 2, respectively:

$$\text{Year 1: } \frac{5,000}{60,000} \times 100 = 8.3\%$$

$$\text{Year 2: } \frac{25,000}{250,000} \times 100 = 10\%$$

The percentage rates of dividend and dividend yield are relevant to an evaluation of the worth of our company as a vehicle for investment. But the data used in the above calculations refer to the company's investment status and profitability as at the date of the last balance sheet. Most investors would try to assess the likelihood of a similar dividend being paid in the next year following upon that balance sheet. In this matter, the dividend cover ratio will be of some guidance. Dividend cover describes the extent to which the year's *post tax profits available for Ordinary shares* has been used to pay that year's ordinary dividends. We can calculate the ratio in the following way:

$$\frac{\text{Post-tax profits available for Ordinary shares}}{\text{Total amount of Ordinary dividend paid in the year}}$$

For each of the two years of the Growing Group's life, the dividend cover ratios would be

$$\text{Year 1: } \frac{14,000}{5,000} = 2.8 \text{ times}$$

$$\text{Year 2: } \frac{62,000}{25,000} = 2.5 \text{ times}$$

The figures show that in year 1, the total dividend could have been paid 2.8 times. In year two it could have been paid 2.5 times. With dividend cover rates such as these the prospects of continuing to receive a dividend of 10 per cent in year 3, look good. The dividend policies that companies operate are seen to vary widely; they will be influenced by the firm's cash needs for financing

1   Increased expenditure on fixed assets.
2   Replacement of fixed assets.
3   Increased investment in working capital.

Thus it is stated that a dividend cover of 1.7 to 1.8 would be a satisfactory rate to maintain, the reader must remember that circumstances such as those noted above may act to vary the relationship between profits available for dividend and the actual dividend paid. The corporate cash flow will have many demands upon it — especially in a period of rapidly rising prices — and it is essential that a company's operating efficiency and credit worthiness are not put at risk as a result of profligate dividend distributions.

Post-tax earning under imputation

From 5 April 1973 a new system of dealing with company tax and with tax on shareholders' dividends came into force. It is called the imputation system and its principal features are

1   Company profits will continue to be liable to Corporation Tax.
2   Shareholders' dividends will continue to be liable to Income Tax at the standard rate.
3   The tax deducted from dividends, when the *net* dividends are paid to shareholders, will be treated as an advance payment of the firm's Corporation Tax (ACT).
4   The tax deducted from dividends will be regarded as part of a *gross* sum received by the shareholder.

Clearly the amount of ACT available to meet future corporation tax liabilities will depend upon the amount of dividends being paid. Furthermore as ACT operates to reduce the amount of corporation tax payable from company funds, then we can say that the post tax earnings of a company are now available to pay net of tax dividends rather than the gross (pre-tax) dividends as was previously the case.

In this chapter our method of determining earnings available for Ordinary shareholders has been based upon

```
Post-tax profits - Other prior dividend
                        (that is, Preference) charges
```

We now have to account for the fact that the amount of equity earnings available for paying dividends is dependent upon the dividend itself. It is therefore imperative to adopt some regular form of calculating equity earnings so that we can continue to appraise the worthwhileness of alternative forms of investment in ordinary shares.

Nil, net and actual earnings

Firstly we can decide that all calculations shall be based upon the assumption that no dividends are being paid. Equity earnings would continue to be calculated as before. This is called the NIL distribution method.

Secondly we can assume that the whole of the post-tax earnings are to be distributed to shareholders. Here the value of the post-tax equity earnings will be increased by the ACT contribution to the corporate tax bill. This is called the FULL distribution method.

The choice between the two methods is not without its complications because ACT must be regarded as an advance of *UK* Corporation Tax. ACT cannot be used as an advance on account of the taxation liability arising from foreign earnings. In order to deal with those situations where ACT cannot be used, either in part or entirely, to meet a firm's taxation debts, we can calculate equity earnings as though ACT was a cost of paying the dividends. In this case we could justifiably use the nil distribution method for earnings, EPS and P/E ratio calculations.

Alternatively, we can regard the unrecovered ACT (that amount which cannot be set off because of the preponderance of foreign earnings) as an additional company tax charge, and reduce the earnings figure by the unrecovered amount. This method is now accepted by the financial press and is termed the NET or ACTUAL method. But we recognise that where a company can recover the whole of its ACT, then there is no difference between the NET and NIL methods so far as earnings-based ratios are concerned. Firms for which full recovery of ACT will not be available include those with

1   Large foreign tax liabilities and/or

2   Below average UK tax liabilities due to heavy capital expenditure allowances against tax.

Earnings and dividend rates

One result of the new system is that companies are declaring the percentage rate of their dividends by reference to the net (post-tax) amounts payable. Nevertheless when we calculate dividend yields we shall continue to use the following formula:

$$\frac{\text{Gross dividend per share x 100}}{\text{Market price per share}}$$

Now dividend cover has been explained (page 131) as the number of times that a gross dividend could be paid from post-tax equity earning. Under the new system the cover ratio will be calculated as follows:

$$\frac{\text{Post-tax equity earnings on a full distribution basis}}{\text{Gross dividends declared}}$$

At the same time the earnings yield ratio will be determined by using the full distribution basis as shown below:

$$\frac{\text{Earnings per Ordinary share on the basis of a full distribution of post-tax earnings}}{\text{Market price per share}} \times 100$$

P/E ratios will be calculated on a NIL basis and, for the special type of company with overseas earnings, a NET basis.

Exhibit 58 shows the effects of the imputation system of taxation upon earnings based ratios. The example presumes a standard rate of income tax of 30 per cent, a company having 5,000 Ordinary shares in issue, and that the market price of the shares is £5 each. Items 6 and 7 in respect of the imputation calculations show that dividend cover and earnings yield are to be based upon full distribution of the profits after tax of £600. In these circumstances £600 would represent the net dividend sum payable to the ordinary shareholders. Therefore the gross dividend belonging to the shareholders will — with the standard rate of income tax of 30 per cent — be

$$\frac{\text{£600 x 100}}{70} = \text{£857}$$

ACT therefore would be £257.

Exhibit 58

EFFECTS OF IMPUTATION ON EARNINGS-BASED RATIOS

Details (1)	Pre-imputation (2)	Imputation (3)
1 Post-tax profits	£600	£600
2 Gross dividend	£450	£450
3 Dividend percentage: gross	9%	9%
4 Dividend percentage: net	6.3%	6.3%
5 Dividend yield (based on gross dividends, for both systems of taxation)	1.8%	1.8%
6 Dividend cover (on a FULL distribution basis for the imputation system)	1.33 times $600/450$	1.9 times $(600 + 257)/450$
7 Earnings yield (on a FULL distribution basis for the imputation system)	2.4% $\dfrac{600 \times 100}{25,000}$	3.43% $\dfrac{(600 + 257) \times 100}{25,000}$
8 EPS on a NIL or NET distribution basis	12p	12p
9 P/E ratio for the imputation system	41.7	41.7

(1) Where the company has most of its income taxed abroad, the EPS and P/E ratios will be calculated on the NET basis. This recognises ACT as an additional company tax charge, in these special circumstances.

(2) Gross dividends are quoted here because the shareholder is deemed to have received the gross sum. Under the imputation system, the dividend shown in the PL account would be recorded as £315 – the amount actually paid. The tax deducted at the time of payment is calculated by taking 30% of £450, i.e. £135, which sum is the amount to be used by the company as an instalment of its liability for Corporation Tax, the ACT referred to in the foregoing pages.

(3) The £25,000 in item 7 derives from 5000 shares in issue having a market price of £5 each.

There is one final point to note in the relationship between the ratios in the table. In the pre-imputation period, the product of the dividend yield, the dividend cover and the P/E ratio equalled 100, thus

```
1.8 x 1.33 x 41.7 = 100
```
(approx. due to decimal points calculation)

This simple relationship no longer applies with the imputation system because dividend cover is based upon a full distribution basis whilst the P/E ratio is derived from a NIL or NET basis,

```
1.8 x 1.9 x 41.7 = 143 (approx.)
```

Inflation and market worth

A note of caution must be sounded about the indiscriminate use of the various dividend, earnings, and related share price ratios when we are evaluating the worth of investments in the ordinary shares of quoted companies. Historically these indexes have been sound bases for the appraisal of corporate worth. At one time dividend cover was the most commonly accepted guide, whilst in recent years the P/E ratio has been the principal yardstick of equity worth. Now it was no mere whim of the financial analyst that generated such changes in preferences for specific appraisal indexes. It was the need to use criteria which were more appropriate to the economic and company taxation conditions of the time, that urged the application of particular appraisal tools in the processes of evaluation.

Therefore the reader will not be surprised to find that the present high rate of inflation (1974/5), has generated yet a fresh approach to the appraisal of corporate worth. Dividend yield has become more important. The percentage rate of dividend yield can be compared with the percentage rate of inflation. In this way the investor can compare his return (dividend) on capital against the rate of inflation and thus seek the most advantageous employment for his funds. Now the investor's chances of combatting the ravages of inflation will be bettered with a high dividend yield which is well covered — a point which has, amongst other things, led to the current preferences for the dividend yield plus cover criteria. The importance of earnings, earnings per share and the P/E ratio as indicators of corporate worth has relevance only in so far as they indicate the extent of dividend cover. Prospective rewards to be gained at some time in the future by use of the retained earnings is not such a powerful appraisal factor in a period of rampant inflation.

These changes have been brought about by rising interest rates on

borrowed money, which themselves have been generated by inflation.
At the same time increased borrowing by industrial and commercial firms has been caused by their incomes being insufficient to cover the increased cost of business operations, costs which have increased through the effects of inflation. Dividend yields have thus been forced up by falling ordinary share values which at the same time have resulted in the related earnings yields being at a considerable premium over those dividend yields. Emphasis is thereby given to the present-day rejection of earnings based ratios as a means of appraising corporate worth. A bird in the hand . . . .

Clearly the financial analyst must adjust his judgement criteria to reflect current business conditions. He should be watchful of other features of a business' operational stability such as:

1   The ratio of long term loans to total shareholders' interest being not more than 40 per cent.
2   The ratio of total liabilities to total shareholders' interest being not more than 60 per cent.
3   A minimum 3 to 1 pre-tax profits cover for interest amounts payable.
4   The maintenance of good profit margins on sales — 10 per cent plus.
5   Profits per employee and per £ of wages paid.
6   The ratio of stock to working capital.

Other guidelines should be devised which will relate to the problems of the trade or industry in which a firm is engaged. But it must be understood that the foregoing strictures on the unsupported use of earnings based ratios derive from the uncertainties of conducting business operations in a period of extreme monetary inflation. A return to more stable economic and monetary conditions will, most likely, see the P/E and earnings yield indexes of worth again being viewed as acceptable measures of corporate worth.

Finally, if dividend yields are vital to the appraisal of corporate worth then the order of priority in payment of the dividends and interests will be a material consideration. The next section of our studies now deals with this aspect of business financing.

Preference shares and loan stock

So far in this chapter we have been appraising the market worth of the company. In particular we reviewed the value of the firm's Ordinary shares from the standpoints of various equity earnings-based ratios. But many companies are financed by other types of long term funds such as preference shares and debentures where fixed dividend/interest rewards are payable. In general the market values of these shares and loan stock will be affected by current long-term interest rates which are being offered on the market. Thus if the long-term interest rate was 12 per cent, we could expect that the market price of the Growing Group's 6 per cent Preference Shares — nominal value £1 — would be about 50p.

Whilst market interest rates are relevant to the valuation of fixed reward capital, we also have to consider the risks which these shares — and debenture holders undertake. Here we can analyse the effects which a specific mix of the various kinds of long term funds can have upon the market worths of the several share and debenture issues which are present in that mix (in reality the reader is about to extend his knowledge of the influence of gearing upon corporate worth). Now it has been stressed that the basic investment worth of Ordinary shares will depend upon the skill with which the firm's management can generate trading profits, and then use some of those profits in the creation of additional corporate wealth. It must also be recognised however, that the worth of an investment in shares or debentures will also be influenced by the value of the company's net tangible assets.

These assets and earnings will be available to reward investors who have subscribed to or purchased the company's shares or debentures. There is nevertheless an order of priority in which the various groups of investors are entitled to be paid their interests or dividends. That order of priority will apply also to the repayment of the capital sums invested, for example, in those circumstances where the company ceases trading. Clearly this order of priority of payment for interest dividend and capital sums must influence the opinions, formed by investors and investment analysts, of the worthwhileness of investing in such shares or debentures especially where the trading viability of the company appears to be in jeopardy.

When the above payments liabilities are listed in a preferential order and this sequential ordering is also expressed in comparative percentage terms, then the extent to which the company is 'covering' its various financing liabilities becomes evident. The following exhibits will demonstrate how this feature is reported. The first, Exhibit 59, aggregates the book value of the net *tangible* assets which represent the basic worth of the shares and debentures in issue: the data have been taken from Exhibit 21.

Exhibit 60 now lists the various types of long-term funds that have financed the firm's acquisition of these assets. The catalogue of funds is presented in an order of priority for repayment with debentures ranking first in the queue and equity last. The 'reserves' element of the funding is not given as £475,000 (the balance sheet

Exhibit 59   *139*

THE GROWING GROUP, YEAR 2: NET TANGIBLE ASSETS

	£
Fixed assets	460,000
Investments	75,000
Current assets	675,000
	1,210,000
Less Current liabilities	410,000
	800,000

figure) because the deduction of

Goodwill	£35,000 and
Capital expenses	£40,000

was necessary to achieve a net *tangible asset* worth of those reserves. The table shows the percentage which each separate financing group forms of the total funds invested.

Thus we can see that the first 12.5 per cent is made up of debentures and the next 6¼ per cent of Preference shares. From this data and the accumulating priority percentages, the analyst could conclude

Exhibit 60

PRIORITY PERCENTAGES I

Details	Sums involved £	Percentage of total	Priority percentage
(1)	(2)	(3)	(4)
6% Debentures	100,000	12.50	0–12.50
6% Preference shares	50,000	6.25	12.50–18.75
Ordinary shares	250,000	31.25	18.75–50.00
Reserves	400,000	50.00	50.00–100
	£800,000		

Exhibit 61

PRIORITY PERCENTAGES II

Details	Priority percentage	Over-all cover
(1)	(2)	(3)
6% Debentures	0-12.50	8 times
6% Preference shares	12.50-18.75	5.3 times
Ordinary shares	18.75-50	2 times

that an investment in the debentures and preference shares of the Growing Group would be reasonably secure because the *book* value of the net tangible assets would have to fall by over 80 per cent before any loss of the relevant capital sums occurred.

The priority percentages dealt with above can also be expressed in terms of an over-all cover. This term described the number of times that the particular segment of the corporate long term funds could be 'paid' out of the net tangible assets. Exhibit 61 gives this information.

Calculation of the over-all cover shown in column 3 is completed in the following way

$$\text{Debentures} = \frac{800,000}{100,000} = 8 \text{ times}$$

When the cover rating for the Preference shares is calculated, then the cumulative total of the debenture stocks plus the Preference shares is divided into the total funds invested:

$$\frac{800,000}{150,000} = 5.3 \text{ times}$$

Priority percentages and annual dividend/interest

An appraisal of the worth of share or debenture holdings will be as much concerned with the priority order for payment of the annual dividend and interest amounts as with the priority ranking for repayment of the capital sums invested. Therefore the methods used in tabulating the data in Exhibits 60 and 61 will now be applied to the annual rewards shown as being paid to the various fund types in year 2 of the Growing Group's profit and loss account (page 90).

With the system of imputation taxation the post-tax profits are regarded as being available to pay the *net* dividends of shareholders. An amount equivalent to the tax payable on the gross dividend is not passed to the shareholder but is retained and used by the company to make advance payments on account of its own Corporation Tax liabilities. Therefore in the following table of priority percentages, net dividends have been used: they were calculated as shown below:

```
Preference shares - Gross dividend      £3,000
                    Tax at 30%             900

                    Net dividend        £2,100

Ordinary shares  -  Gross dividend     £25,000
                    Tax at 30%           7,500

                    Net dividend       £17,500
```

Exhibit 62 lists the post-tax costs of the dividend interest payments made by the Growing Group in year 2. The reader must note that debenture interest is an expense which is an allowable charge against income before Corporation Tax is assessed. Dividends on the

Exhibit 62

PRIORITY PERCENTAGES III

```
                                          £
Post-tax profits (per Exhibit 38)      65,000
Post-tax costs of Debenture interest    3,000

Amount available for post-tax
    dividend/interest payments        £68,000
```

Details	Net dividends and interest £	Priority percentages	Over-all cover
(1)	(2)	(3)	(4)
Debentures	3,000	0-4.4	Over 22 times
Preference shares	2,100	4.4-7.5	Over 13 times
Ordinary shares	17,500	7.5-33.2	Over 3 times
Balance	45,400		
	£68,000		

other hand, are paid from and charged against post tax profits. It becomes necessary therefore, when priority percentages are being evaluated, to ensure that the sums involved are quoted in comparable terms, i.e. post-tax costs. In this case, as the total charge for debenture interest was £6,000, then the post-tax interest cost (with a 50 per cent tax charge) would be £3,000. With this adjustment in mind the exhibit will show the relevant priority percentages and cover for each payment.

The above priority percentages and cover shown in Exhibit 62 relate to the actual dividends declared and the post-tax profits reported in the profit and loss account. No attempt has been made to 'gross up' the post-tax profits to account for the ACT which would become available, either with the above level of dividends or with a full distribution of available earnings. The question of companies with profits taxed abroad, and therefore not in a position to recover the whole of ACT, would be dealt by increasing the tax charge.

Further reading

A.P. Robson, *Essential accounting for managers,* Cassell (1966).

E.M. Lerner, *Managerial finance,* Harcourt Brace (1971). (See especially Chapters 1-5).

H. Bierman, *Financial accounting theory,* Macmillan (1965). (See especially Chapters 5-7).

J.L. Brown and R.L. Howard, *Principles of management accountancy,* MacDonald & Evans (1965). (See especially Part 4 - Information for Management Control).

E.A. Helfert, *Techniques of financial analysis,* Irwin (Second edition).

H.A. Edey, 'True and fair view', *Accountancy,* p 440 (August 1971).

M. Greener, 'The definition of profits', *Certified Accountant,* pp 39-41 (January/February 1974).

'Calculating the return on capital employed', *Accountant,* pp 841-44 (4 June 1970).

R.G. Bassett, 'Return on investment', *ibid.* (6 April 1972).

Accounting for Inflation | 5

Introduction

For many years accountants, economists and lawyers have recognised that an unstable monetary unit impedes realistic financial analyses of corporate worth and profitability, where those analyses rely upon data recorded in conventional balance sheets and profit and loss accounts. Moreover it is now accepted that reporting the results of business activities in historic cost terms — which is the basis of conventional balance sheets and profit and loss accounts — does not provide financial data which are accurate enough for effective business planning. The impacts of inflation upon pricing and financing structures, costs of production, dividend policies and liquidity states must be quantitatively assessed and brought to account, if we are to achieve well-grounded appraisals of corporate worth and performance from year to year.

It can be seen quite readily that the monetary values attributed to certain items in conventional accounting statements will present inaccurate information when the effects of inflation are ignored. The monetary worths given to fixed assets, to annual depreciation charges, valuations of stock and to the costs of debt financing are cases in point. We have shown already that historic cost accounting fails to deal objectively with these particular problems. We know that some companies revalue their fixed assets from time to time or they make supplementary provisions for asset depreciation in order to give some notion of the extent of change in the corporate worth and its costs of operation.

But such adjustments as these are based upon subjective opinion about the movement in, for example, fixed asset purchase prices, just as though exactly the same assets would be available — or desired — for immediate replacement in a continuing business. Clearly, we must recognise that the effects of inflation upon statements of income and of net worth will be more far reaching than would be reflected in revaluations of fixed assets and depreciation charges alone.

Current purchasing power

When dealing with the data in successive financial statements, within an inflationary environment, we have to recognise that today's £ is a different £ from that found in previous years. Though each of the units of one £ will have the same numerical significance when balance sheets and profit and loss accounts are constructed, each year's individual *real* worths will be vastly different. A £ of the earlier period(s) was able to command ownership and use of more or better physical resources than the £ of today. In other words the value of the currency unit has fallen: it cannot purchase the same amount of goods and services as it formerly did.

Such a situation will be aggravated by the continuance of inflation over a long period. This can soon make it impossible to identify a *current real* worth of corporate activities, merely by studying annual financial statements. Comparisons of company wealth and income over several years become difficult to say the least. Comparisons between different companies could be meaningless since (a) their patterns of growth and (b) the composition of their net worths will be affected differently by diverse yearly rates of inflation. We need to have a currency conversion index which will bring the £'s of separate accounting periods into a common current worth. Such a conversion process will be similar to that used by companies who have trading units in foreign countries. When the net wealths and incomes of overseas trading establishments are brought into a UK firm's balance sheet and profit and loss account, the foreign currency items are converted into sterling by using international currency exchange rates.

When accounting for inflation however the conversion index to be used should be the Consumer Price Index which is calculated annually by the Central Statistical Office. However, *annual* compilation has its problems: all companies do not prepare final accounts ending on 31 December in each year and therefore a monthly conversion index will be required also, in order to accommodate the various accounting year-ends and other inter-year transactions. To meet these needs, the monthly Index of Retail Prices produced by the Department of Employment is available.

The aim of using the above indices is to prepare supplementary value adjusted balance sheets and profit and loss accounts from final accounts based upon historic cost principles. Historic cost annual accounts will continue to be produced, but the separate supplementary statements will then demonstrate the effects of an unstable monetary unit upon those corporate worths and incomes which are recorded in the conventional accounts. Essentially the conversion indices represent movements in the general purchasing power of the currency unit. The method seeks to present (a series of) balance sheets and income statements containing monetary values which are realistically comparable.

The conversion index

An example of the use of a general purchasing power index is given below. Exhibit 63 sets out the fixed asset purchases of two firms A and B over a period of three years, during which time the index of purchasing power was as shown in column 4.

In conventional balance sheets the gross costs of the fixed assets would be shown as £6,000 at 31 December Year 3, for both firms. If we now wish to convert the historical cost pounds for the above assets into general purchasing power pounds as at 31 December Year 3, the following calculations will be necessary:

1 Each asset's purchase cost must be multiplied by the index rating at the date of the proposed supplementary statement. i.e. 31 December Year 3.
2 The sum resulting from (1) must be divided by the index rating at the date of the original transaction.

Exhibit 64 gives the appropriate details.

The revised price adjusted figures show clearly that Firm B possesses assets of a greater real worth than Firm A. This is because

Exhibit 63

FIXED ASSET PURCHASES - HISTORICAL COST

Dates of purchases	Costs of fixed assets purchased		Conversion index
	Firm A £	Firm B £	
(1)	(2)	(3)	(4)
1 Jan: Year 1	1,000	3,000	100
1 Jan: Year 2	2,000	2,000	110
1 Jan: Year 3	3,000	1,000	120
31 Dec: Year 3	–	–	130

more of Firm B's assets were acquired before the monetary unit began to lose its purchasing power. Furthermore if the expected economic lives of the assets were 10 years for both firms, and each had used the straight line method of calculating depreciation, then the historical cost depreciation charge would be £600 for each firm (£6,000)/10 in Year 3. With a similar depreciation policy, depreciation charges in Year 3 would be

Firm A   £691

Firm B   £734

in the supplementary statements based upon general purchasing power indices.

A comparison of the balance sheet entries for these two firms' fixed assets is given in Exhibit 65. The extracts based upon historical cost would result in identical initial cost figures for the stocks of fixed assets in both firms. However, different timings of the various acquisitions must result in different aggregate depreciation amounts at the end of Year 3, in the historical cost accounts. Exhibit 65 shows these impacts upon the net book values of fixed assets and the reader will appreciate their resultant effects upon the book worth of the capital employed sums. The exhibit goes on to show how the accumulation of annual depreciation charges in respect of the several fixed assets

1   Leads to calculation of the historical total depreciation charges at the end of Year 3, (column 4) and

2   Is used to convert the above historical total depreciation charges

Exhibit 64

147

FIXED ASSET PURCHASES - AT CURRENT PURCHASING
POWER, 31 DECEMBER YEAR 3

Date of purchase	Firm A		Firm B	
	Price level adjustments	Revised value,£	Price level adjustments	Revised value,£
1 Jan: Year 1	$1000 \times \dfrac{130}{100}$	1,300	$3000 \times \dfrac{130}{100}$	3,900
1 Jan: Year 2	$2000 \times \dfrac{130}{110}$	2,364	$2000 \times \dfrac{130}{110}$	2,364
1 Jan: Year 3	$3000 \times \dfrac{130}{120}$	3,250	$1000 \times \dfrac{130}{120}$	1,083
Revised totals as at 31 Dec: Year 3	£6,914		£7,347	

into pounds of current purchasing power at the end of Year 3 (column 8).

Calculation of the inflation adjusted annual depreciation charges and aggregate depreciation sums are completed in exactly the same way as inflation adjustment examples in Exhibit 64.

These exhibits present simple examples of the application of a conversion index to a single section of a company's balance sheet. In addition to impacts upon quantification of net worth, the consequent changes in annual depreciation charges will affect the profit or loss revealed by the supplementary, price adjusted, income statement. Furthermore the process of converting historical cost data to their current purchasing power equivalents will involve adjustments to assets of different types as well as to the firm's liabilities also. Here we have to appreciate the varying effects which the possession of (a) monetary and (b) non-monetary assets and liabilities will generate for corporate wealth and income, in an inflationary environment.

Now monetary items comprise cash, debtors, creditors and loans whilst non-monetary items include physical assets such as stock, plant, machinery, vehicles, equipment and buildings. The numerical size of monetary items is fixed in terms of the (historical) pounds in which they were originally expressed, This means that the holder of monetary assets loses purchasing power in a period of inflation.

Exhibit 65

Balance Sheet Data of Fixed Assets as at 31 December, Year 3

DETAILS	HISTORIC COST				CURRENT PURCHASING POWER		
	Asset initial cost	Year 3 depreciation charge	Aggregate depreciation at 31 Dec Year 3	Index at date of acquisition	Price-level adjusted value Exhibit 64	Adjusted Year 3 depreciation charge	Adjusted aggregate depreciation at 31 Dec Year 3
	(2)	(3)	(4)	(5)	(6)	(7)	(8)
	£	£	£		£	£	£
FIRM A							
Year 1	1,000	100	300	100	1,300	130	390
Year 2	2,000	200	400	110	2,364	236	473
Year 3	3,000	300	300	120	3,250	325	325
	£6,000	£600	£1,000		£6,914	£691	£1,188
FIRM B							
Year 1	3,000	300	900	100	3,900	390	1,170
Year 2	2,000	200	400	110	2,364	236	473
Year 3	1,000	100	100	120	1,083	108	108
	£6,000	£600	£1,400		£7,347	£734	£1,751

Balance Sheet Book Value 31 Dec Year 3 (FIRM A)   £6,000 – £1,000 = £5,000

Inflation-adjusted Balance Sheet Value 31 Dec Year 3 (FIRM A)   £6,914 – £1,188 = £5,726

Balance Sheet Book Value 31 Dec Year 3 (FIRM B)   £6,000 – £1,400 = £4,600

Inflation-adjusted Balance Sheet Value 31 Dec Year 3 (FIRM B)   £7,347 – £1,751 = £5,596

Conversely those having monetary liabilities will gain purchasing power since delay in settlement of any liability results in payments being made in lower valued pounds.

At the same time we must realise that the possession of non-monetary assets during a period of inflation, does not earn an inflationary 'profit'. The values given to these assets in the supplementary statements reflect proportionate changes in the monetary worths, consequent upon the rate of inflation operating since the assets were purchased. The possessor of non-monetary assets merely maintains his physical wealth as a result of having exchanged a monetary asset (cash) for a non-monetary asset (plant) before the fall in value of the monetary unit made the asset acquisition more costly in monetary terms.

Practical examples

The next series of exhibits demonstrates the conversion of final account data from a historical cost basis to a general purchasing power basis of reporting. Firstly, balance sheets at the beginning and end of a year must be expressed in the general purchasing power values existing at the end of the year, i.e: at the date of the second balance sheet. Secondly, items in the profit and loss account will be similarly adjusted to take note of the changes in the purchasing power index during the year. Exhibit 66 details the movements of the index over a six-year period and gives values of the index for certain periods during the year. Appropriate index ratings from this exhibit are used in the conversion process.

Exhibits 67 and 68 are directed to a consideration of the firm's position at the end of year 4 and explanations of the adjustments are given below, starting with the non-monetary assets.

Fixed assets

It has been assumed that a single fixed asset was acquired by XYZ Limited on 1 January Year 1. At that time its purchase price was £1,000 and the purchasing power index stood at 100. Because the appraisal relates to the situation at the end of year 4 when the conversion index had reached 122, the required conversion calculation will be

$$£1,000 \times \frac{122}{100} = £1,220$$

Exhibit 66

CONSUMER PRICE INDEX

Year	At commencement of the year	Average for the year	At commencement of final quarter of the year	Average for the final quarter of the year	At end of the year
1	100	102.5	103.8	104.4	105
2	105	107.5	108.8	109.4	110
3	110	113.0	114.5	115.2	116
4	116	119.0	120.5	121.2	122
5	122	125.0	126.5	127.2	128
6	128	131.0	132.5	133.2	134

Exhibit 67

XYZ COMPANY LIMITED

Balance sheet as at 31 December, Year 3

	Historic cost details		Price level adjusted details			
	£	£	x	÷	£	£
Fixed assets at cost		1,000	122	100		1,220
Less Depreciation		400	122	100		488
TOTAL FIXED ASSETS		600				732
Current assets						
Stock	330		122	115.2	349	
Debtors	350		122	116	368	
Cash	120		122	116	126	
	800				843	
Less Current liabilities						
Creditors	350		122	116	368	
NET CURRENT ASSETS		450				475
TOTAL SHAREHOLDERS' FUNDS		£1,050				£1,207

Exhibit 68

XYZ COMPANY LIMITED

Balance sheet as at 31 December, Year 4

	Historic cost details		Price level adjusted details				
	£	£	x	÷	£	£	£
Fixed assets at cost		1,000				122	100		1,220
Less Depeciation		500	122	100			610
TOTAL FIXED ASSETS		500					610
Current assets							
Stock	440		122	121.2	443		
Debtors	550				550		
Cash	250				250		
	1,240				1,243		
Less Current liabilities							
Creditors	290				290		
NET CURRENT ASSETS		950					953
TOTAL SHAREHOLDERS' FUNDS		£1,450					£1,563

Now in order to compare the firm's wealth at Year 3 with that at Year 4, both balance sheets must show the purchasing power value of the fixed asset as £1,220. If several assets had been acquired at various times during a year then the appropriate index to be used, in place of 100 in the above equation, would be the *average* index rating for the year in question. For example if the expenditure of £1,000 related to a number of assets acquired *during* year 1, the conversion equation would have been

$$£1,000 \times \frac{122}{102.5} = £1,190$$

Depreciation

Historical cost depreciation is shown as £400 and £500 for years 3 and 4, respectively. These amounts result from using the straight line depreciation method in conjunction with an expected 10-year economic life for the asset involved. Conversion of these aggregate depreciation amounts will follow the same principles as those applied to the purchase price of the asset. Therefore to bring data in both balance sheets to a common general purchasing power position at the end of year 4, our calculations must be

$$£400 \times \frac{122}{100} = £488$$

$$£500 \times \frac{122}{100} = £610$$

The first important point for comparative analysis now emerges — the general purchasing power value of the fixed assets declines from £732 to £610, whereas the historic cost data shows a fall from £600 to £500. The percentage fall is the same in both cases BUT the monetary value of the firm's net worth and its capital employed will be more realistically quoted in the supplementary adjusted statement. We shall have to watch the impacts of these (and other) revised figures upon ROC, etc.: subsequent exhibits will help us to do this.

In a practical situation, conversion of asset cost prices and their relevant depreciation sums will involve more detailed calculations than the above. The simplicity of the basic method remains: but it has to be applied to the year by year historic cost data of all of the assets presently possessed by the company. Monetary values of yearly acquisitions, disposals and related depreciation sums must be converted to the current general purchasing power index. It is the work involved, not the method, which increases in complexity.

The stock values in both balance sheets have to be converted to purchasing power equivalents. For this purpose we shall assume that the physical stock on hand at the end of any year, was acquired during the last quarter of that year. Consequently the conversion indices relating to the date of acquisition of these non-monetary assets will be the index's *average* rating during the appropriate final quarter. Thus the adjustment for year 3 stock will be

$$£330 \times \frac{122}{115.2} = £349$$

and for year 4

$$£440 \times \frac{122}{121.2} = £443$$

Before we leave the subject of current purchasing power values for stock, it must be emphasised that the basic stock valuation principle of 'lower of cost or net realisable value' is NOT to be ignored. Adjusted purchasing power values for stocks will be entered in the supplementary statements just so long as they do NOT exceed the expected net realisable values of that stock. In such an instance (purchasing power values being higher than NRV) the supplementary statements would show stock at its expected net realisable value.

Monetary items

To complete our conversion of the two balance sheets to current purchasing power values, we turn to the monetary items. Now each of these monetary items is deemed to have been 'acquired'* at the date of the balance sheet in which it is recorded, and consequently no changes to the year 4 values will be necessary. On the other hand the values of monetary items in the year 3 balance sheet must be converted by reference to the index obtaining at that date. The calculation applied to the year 3 debtors is as follows

$$£350 \times \frac{122}{116} = £368$$

Exhibit 67 shows the monetary items being calculated individually. This is not essential, for the same index ratings apply to each of the

*In fact we are expressing the values attributed to these monetary items in their respective balance sheets, in terms of their current purchasing power.

debtors, cash and creditors. One calculation to convert the *net* monetary assets' value would have sufficed.

Total shareholders' interest

The net effect of the various conversion adjustments to monetary and non-monetary items is now reflected in the book value of the Total Shareholders' Interest (net worth). Here it is vital to note that the constituent parts of net worth — issued shares, reserves and profit and loss account balances — are NOT adjusted by the application of conversion indices. (It must be pointed out that some authorities do recommend adjustment of, for example, Ordinary share capital by reference to changes in the index since the share issue was made: an evaluation of the current purchasing power of the shareholders' original capital invested is thereby made.) The figure of net worth shown in a supplementary purchasing power adjusted balance sheet is derived simply by deducting the other liabilities from the assets when those other liabilities and assets have been converted to general purchasing power pounds, at the date of the statement.

Profit and loss account

The final stages in the conversion process are recorded in Exhibits 69 and 70. Again we have as our objective the conversion of each group of historic costs, in the profit and loss account, into their year end equivalent purchasing power values. Thus if we start with sales, and assume that the transactions had occurred evenly throughout the year, then the 'time of transaction' index to be used would be the average rating for the year. In such circumstances the conversion calculation will be, as is given in Exhibit 69

$$£3,150 \times \frac{122}{119} = £3,229$$

If we can identify a spasmodic sales pattern, it would be better to deal with the sales, quarter by quarter, in our conversion calculations. Here we would have to determine an average rating of the purchasing power index for each of the separate quarters. All that this means is that there would be four computations for the year's sales, instead of the one given above.

Exhibit 69

XYZ COMPANY LIMITED

Profit and Loss Account for Year 4

	£	£	x	÷	£	£
Sales		3,150	122	119		3,229
Stock at 1 Jan	330		122	115.2	349	
Purchases	2,000		122	119	2,050	
	2,330				2,399	
Less Stock at 31 Dec	440		122	121.2	443	
Cost of goods sold		1,890				1,956
Gross profit		1,260				1,273
Less						
Administration and selling expenses	760		122	119	779	
Depreciation	100		(10% x £1,220)		122	
Monetary items	–	860			16	917
Net profit		£400				£356

Gain or loss on monetary items

One item in the supplementary profit and loss account requires further examination. It is the charge of £16 being 'borne' by XYZ and which results from holding monetary items during a year when the purchasing power of the monetary unit was declining. Clearly a holder of cash loses wealth in a period of inflation: his money possessions will buy less and less as inflation continues. For the same reasons granting credit to customers results in a loss of purchasing power, whilst the amounts due remain unpaid. Conversely, the receipt of credit facility from a supplier will act to the benefit of the recipient, when inflation is rife.

Thus we have to measure the costs of being a holder of net monetary assets and Exhibit 70 details the calculations necessary for this purpose.

The exhibit shows that XYZ started the year with net monetary assets of £120, and to this extent the firm was liable to lose purchasing

Exhibit 70   157

LOSS OF PURCHASING POWER DURING YEAR 4 FROM HOLDING NET MONETARY ASSETS

	Historic cost details £	Adjusted for price level changes £
1 January		
Debtors	350	368
Cash	120	126
	470	494
Less Creditors	350	368
Net monetary assets	120	126
Receipts		
Sales	3,150	3,229
	£3,270	£3,355
Less: Payments		
Purchases	2,000	2,050
Expenses	760	779
	£2,760	£2,829
Difference	510	526
31 December		
Debtors	550	550
Cash	250	250
	800	800
Creditors	290	290
	£510	£510
Loss of purchasing power		16

power in the inflationary environment. During the year, monetary assets flowed to the company from the sales of £3,150. At the same time the outflow of monetary assets to meet the costs of operations were £2,760. The arithmetical result of the opening state of £120, adjusted for subsequent inflows and outflows, indicates a net monetary asset position at the end of year 4 of £510. This is confirmed by the debtors, cash and creditor amounts recorded in year 4 balance sheet.

Now, when the historical cost data are converted to pounds of current purchasing power at 31 December Year 4, we find that the net monetary asset position *ought* to be £526 if no loss of purchasing power was to be suffered. But since the net monetary asset state at the year end is shown to be £510, then a loss of purchasing power of £16 is established. This is the amount recorded in the supplementary profit and loss statement given in Exhibit 69.

Future years

The above exhibits give an introduction to a recommended method of accounting for inflation, though more detailed matters of practice have been omitted in order to give emphasis and reason to the relatively simple principles involved. The next stage examines the preparation of supplementary statements in the years ahead after the major tasks, involved in the first of such statements, have been completed. Clearly, when the first inflation adjusted statements are being prepared a considerable amount of 'once only' research and analysis will be necessary. Past records of fixed asset acquisitions and disposals have to be scrutinised in order to determine the current purchasing power equivalents of the existing fixed asset stock. In a subsequent year these purchasing power equivalent values will be merely updated by relevant conversion indices applicable to the year-end accounting date of the later statement. In addition, continuing programmes of asset acquisitions and disposals will have to be recorded in working papers which support the inflation adjusted accounts. The data will be stored in readily usable form and further time consuming research will not be necessary.

Balance sheets

To instance the updating of supplementary statements, we now return to Exhibit 64. Purchasing power equivalent values were given to the fixed assets of two firms: these values were £6,914 and £7,347 for firms A and B respectively at the end of year 3. Therefore if we prepared inflation adjusted statements for 31 December year 4, taking the index at that date to be 140 and assuming no changes in the physical assets, the inflation adjusted asset values would be

Firm A   £6,914 x $\frac{140}{130}$ = £7,446

Firm B   £7,347 x $\frac{140}{130}$ = £7,912

Furthermore the depreciation charges in the adjusted year 4 profit and loss accounts would be £745 and £791 for A and B, respectively. The reader must recognise that, in assessing the effects of inflation during year 4, the balance sheets at the beginning and at the end of the year will *both* be expressed in the purchasing power values obtaining at the end of year 4.

We can pursue the example further by assuming that the following fixed asset purchases were made, by the two firms, on 1 July Year 4 when the conversion index stood at 135

Firm A   £1,500

Firm B   £1,000

These additions to the fixed asset stocks will be included in the supplementary statements at the end of Year 4 at the values shown below

Firm A   £1,500 x $\frac{140}{135}$ = £1,556

Firm B   £1,000 x $\frac{140}{135}$ = £1,037

and the new inflation adjusted figures for fixed assets as at 31 December, Year 4 would be

Firm A   £9,002

Firm B   £8,989

Depreciation charges for year 4 will depend upon the firm's policy towards

1   Not charging depreciation in the year of acquisition of an asset.
2   Charging depreciation for the proportion of a full year that the assets were available for use.

We can apply the above principles to the accounts of XYZ as shown in Exhibits 68 and 69. All of the items in the next (year 5) historical cost balance sheet would have to be adjusted to their purchasing power equivalents as at 31 December. Appropriate conversion indices must be used for this purpose. Now, just as we have a series of historic cost balance sheets which purport to show the variations in corporate wealth over the years, so we can present a series of supplementary statements based upon a common general purchasing power index. (In practice the published accounts of companies will show supplementary statements for the two most recent years only). The point to note about a series of current purchasing power statements is that the historical cost data for each year's balance sheet must be expressed in the pounds of current purchasing power obtaining at the end of the last account period. For XYZ this means that the supplementary balance sheets for years 4 and 5 will have their figures adjusted by reference to the purchasing power index of the monetary unit, as at the end of year 5. Comparisons can then be made between two statements of corporate net wealth, in the knowledge that both statements report the situations in terms of a monetary unit with a common purchasing power rating.

Profit and loss accounts

A profit and loss account for the operations of XYZ during year 5 should be converted by the same methods as those displayed for the year 4 account. Furthermore the net gain or net loss arising during year 5 from the effects of inflation on the firm, due to its holdings of net monetary liabilities or net monetary assets, must also be calculated.

When this is done a series of general purchasing power adjusted profit and loss accounts can be presented. They will show the impact of inflation upon the firm's reported incomes, over a period of years. It is emphasised that, as with the supplementary balance sheets, the series of supplementary profit and loss accounts must have their data expressed in pounds of current purchasing power relating to the last account in the series. In other words the inflation adjusted profit in the supplementary statement for year 4 will be updated by reference to the general purchasing power of the monetary unit at the end of year 5.

Published accounts

The foregoing method of adjusting historic-cost based accounts to take account of changes in the purchasing power of the monetary unit, is based upon recommendations of the Accounting Standards Steering Committee. These recommendations are expressed in the Committee's Exposure Draft No. 8. [Now a provisional statement of standard accounting practice (PSSAP7)].

As yet it is not mandatory for firms to adopt the recommendations or to publish the results even if they accept the recommendations.

Nevertheless certain forward looking companies are publishing appropriate supplementary statements and explanatory notes in their annual report and accounts booklets.

Currys Limited

The 47th Annual Report and Accounts issued by the Directors of Currys Limited reveals that the company operates its retailing business through 406 stores and 5 retail warehouses. Its capital investment in freehold and leasehold properties, fixtures, fittings and machinery is therefore of considerable value even when quoted in depreciated book values based upon historic cost. Furthermore the stocks of retail goods — valued at £13.09m — supported a group turnover of £86.4m during the year under review. Therefore with such a large investment in fixed assets and working stocks, one would expect that a high rate of inflation would have a marked effect upon the firm's net wealth and income.

Recognising this, the company decided to identify the inflationary element in their annual statements of wealth and income. They have consequently prepared supplementary statements in the form recommended and have published these with the 1974 Annual Report and Accounts. The first of these statements is given in Exhibit 71.

The ratios quoted at the foot of the statement are derived (a) from historical cost data and (b) from accounts based upon pounds of current purchasing power. Comparison of these two sets of ratios give sharp emphasis to the effects which inflation has had upon the firm's conventionally reported financial position and profitability. But whilst absolute values of the ratios quoted are of importance to our study, it will be more appropriate to examine the *rates of change* in the company's fortunes. The measurement of the rates of change in the firm's wealth and profitability — as revealed by the two reporting bases — is now shown in Exhibit 72.

Accounting for inflation shows that, during the past year, the real rates of Currys' EPS and Return on Equity Investment have fallen by a much greater proportion than that shown in the (misleading) historical cost accounts. Also the increases in corporate wealth expressed in Net Assets per Share, is greatly overstated by conventional accounting practices. Now it is pointed out that such experiences as these will not be confined to Currys Limited. Those UK companies having similar patterns of investments in fixed assets and stocks, etc., will be similarly affected but the precise extent of the impact of inflation has to be assessed separately for each company.

Finally Exhibit 73 specifies in some detail the causes of the

Exhibit 71

CURRYS LIMITED AND SUBSIDIARY COMPANIES

Summary of Results and Financial Position - adjusted for the effects of inflation - for the year ended 31 January 1974

| | Historical cost basis | | | Current purchasing power basis (1974 pounds) | | |
	1973 £000	1974 £000		1974 £000	1973 £000
Results for the Year					
Cash takings	67,642	86,443		91,227	78,435
Group profit before taxation	6,863	7,767		7,177	7,367
Taxation	2,752	3,878		3,878	3,081
Group profit after taxation	4,111	3,889		3,299	4,286
Surplus on sale of properties	348	92		(27)	131
Group profit available	4,459	3,981		3,272	4,417

	814	748	749	912
Dividends				
Group profit unappropriated	3,645	3,233	2,523	3,505

Financial Position at End of Year

	814	748	749	912
Net current assets	8,719	11,362	11,602	9,841
Fixed assets *less* Depreciation	11,168	12,497	19,033	17,935
	19,887	23,859	30,635	27,776
Less: Preference shares	(660)	(660)	(660)	(739)
Deferred taxation	(2,705)	(3,444)	(3,444)	(3,029)
	16,522	19,755	26,531	24,008

Ratios

Earnings per share	17.4p	16.5p	14.0p	18.2p
Dividend cover	5.3	5.4	4.5	4.9
Return on equity interest	24.6%	19.5%	12.3%	17.6%
Net assets per share	71.0p	84.8p	113.9p	103.1p

Exhibit 72

CURRYS LIMITED AND SUBSIDIARY COMPANIES

Ratio Analysis - 1973 and 1974

	Historical cost basis			Current purchasing power basis		
	1973	1974	Change*	1973	1974	Change*
Earnings per share	17.4p	16.5p	-5.2%	18.2p	14.0p	-23%
Return on equity investment	24.6%	19.5%	-20.7%	17.6%	12.3%	-30.1%
Net assets per share	71.0p	84.8p	+19.4%	103.1p	113.9p	+10.5%

*Percentage change

Exhibit 73

CURRYS LIMITED AND SUBSIDIARY COMPANIES

Analysis of the Effects of Inflation on the Profit and Loss Account

Group Profit Unappropriated (Historical basis)

Adjustments to convert to Current Purchasing Power Basis:

Stocks
   Additional charge based upon restating stocks at the
   beginning and end of year in current purchasing power £s
Depreciation
   Additional depreciation based on cost of fixed assets
   measured in current purchasing power £s
Monetary Items
   Net gain in purchasing power resulting from effects of
   inflation on company's net monetary liabilities
Sales, purchases and all other costs
   These are increased by the change in the index between
   the average date at which they occurred and end of year
Surplus on sale of properties
   Reduction of surplus measured by relating sales proceeds
   to costs in current purchasing power £s
Transfer to Inflation Reserve

Group Profit Unappropriated (at current purchasing power
   £s at end of 1974 and 1973, respectively)
   Adjustment required to update 1973 profit from 1973 to
   1974 £s

Group Profit Unappropriated (1974 £s)

variations in unappropriated profit, as reported in the conversion of historic-cost-based accounts to accounts based upon pounds of current purchasing power.

The reader should notice that the unappropriated profits of £3,130,000 at the end of 1973 is expressed in 1973 pounds. The index at that time was 171.3. In order to bring these figures into a correct updated relationship with the 1974 unappropriated profits, we have to note that the index at the end of 1974 was 191.8. The relevant calculation would then be

$$£3,130 \times \frac{191.8}{171.3} = £3,505$$

As a result of the directors' appreciation of the impacts of inflation upon Currys financial state, they have prudently created an Inflation Reserve. Transfers are made each year to this Reserve 'to take cognisance of the effects of inflation on the Company's Accounts and to mark the fact that this part of the Group Profit cannot prudently be distributed by way of dividends'.

	1974 £000		1973 £000
	3,233		3,645
843		515	
267		154	
(396)		(177)	
(123)		(208)	
119		231	
	——		——
	710		515
	2,523		3,130
	–		375
	£2,523		£3,505

Exhibits 74 and 75 are taken from the Annual Report and Accounts for 1973, issued by the directors of Guest Keen and Nettlefolds Limited. They show, in a form similar to that employed by Currys Limited, the effects of inflation upon the company's reported financial position at the end of 1973, and the net income for that year.

GKN do not make transfers to an Inflation Reserve Account but the dividends paid appear to leave adequate retained profits to preserve the integrity of the equity interest and the stability of this well known company. The reader will find a comparison of Exhibits 73 and 75 to be of interest: the necessary stockholding of raw materials, work-in-progress and finished goods in GKN Limited have a relatively greater impact on the inflation-adjusted profits than did the retail stocks in the accounts of Currys. Other items for comparison can be selected by the earnest student, Exhibit 76 being an example of the approach to follow.

Further thoughts on accounting for inflation

The current purchasing power method of accounting for inflation has been widely acknowledged. A number of UK companies are now presenting supplementary inflation-adjusted balance sheets and profit and loss statements in their annual report and accounts booklets. Clearly, an informed approach to a regular system of accounting for inflation must prevail for the present system of basing annual financial statements upon the historical cost concept is unsatisfactory for a realistic reporting of corporate wealth and income.

But early experiences of statements based on current purchasing power shows that analysts and investors have to make some adjustments to their standards of appraisal of corporate activities. The level of profits revealed in inflation-adjusted accounts will, in most cases, be lower than that in the conventional accounts. Some earnings per share ratios, and the related share value estimations, may well be set at lower levels. If this should happen then there could be a material readjustment in the quantity and mix of new capital money investment for UK industrial and commercial firms.

These comments must depend upon the state of the market, which itself is influenced by factors other than business trading results. Nevertheless it becomes imperative that *all* companies publish inflation-adjusted statements so that comparisons of wealth and profitability may be more realistically founded, throughout UK

Exhibit 74

GUEST, KEEN AND NETTLEFOLDS LIMITED

Accounting for Inflation Statement

Results for the Year	1973		1972
	As published	Adjusted for inflation	Updated in terms of current £s at 29 Dec 1973
	£m	£m	£m
Turnover	819.46	869.23	744.65
Profit for the year before taxation	70.55	66.38	50.89
Taxation	(39.28)	(40.72)	(25.40)
Net profit for the year	31.27	25.66	25.49
Attributable to outside shareholders	3.00	3.13	3.27
Net profit attributable to Ordinary shareholders	28.27	22.53	22.22
Dividends	9.95	9.95	11.90
Profit for the year retained	18.32	12.58	10.32
Financial position at end of year:			
Fixed assets	209.83	293.43	286.65
Investments	103.19	96.67	74.91
Current assets	415.70	419.76	383.11
Current liabilities	(263.14)	(263.14)	(202.40)
Total net assets employed	465.58	546.72	542.27
Deferred liabilities	(35.37)	(35.37)	(30.23)
Medium and long-term indebtedness	(66.08)	(66.08)	(76.05)
Outside shareholders' interest in subsidiaries	(19.11)	(27.43)	(25.89)
Equity interest	345.02	417.84	410.10

Exhibit 75

GUEST, KEEN AND NETTLEFOLDS LIMITED

Details	1973 £m	1973 £m	1972 £m	1972 £m
Profits before taxation as published		70.55		50.51
Adjustments to Current Purchasing Power Basis:				
Stocks	(13.62)		(11.51)	
Depreciation	(2.81)		(2.15)	
Sales, purchses and other costs	2.55		3.10	
Results of Associated Companies	3.44		1.15	
Net gain on monetary liabilities	6.27		2.80	
		(4.17)		(6.61)
Profit before taxation (after accounting for inflation at the end of the year under review)		66.38		43.90
Adjustments to update 1972 figures as originally computed to current £s at 29 December 1973:				
Variation in inflation indices			4.48	
Variation in currency exchange rates			2.51	
				6.99
		66.38		50.89

Exhibit 76

GUEST, KEEN AND NETTLEFOLDS LIMITED

Ratio Analysis - 1972 and 1973

Ratios	Historical cost basis			Current purchasing power basis		
	1972	1973	Change*	1972	1973	Change*
EPS	25.6p	27.2p	+6.2%	21.4p	21.7p	+1.4%
Return on equity investment	9.2%	8.2%	-10.9%	5.4%	5.4%	-

*Percentage change

industrial and commercial life. The ensuing greater understanding of the impacts of inflation upon costs of production, of stockholding and of giving credit to customers, etc., may well lead to price increases from firms who have come to recognise their unrealistic profitability and related cash flow states. Levels of gearing may change when company managers evaluate the real costs of debt finance, with fixed annual interest charges obtaining during a period of falling money values. (Unless the costs of servicing debt become linked to the Consumer Price Index!). The effects upon the corporate cost of capital could be complex. It should be noted however that falling equity share prices must result in a higher cost of capital where firms are financed solely by equity. Industrial development, modernisation and expansion could thereby be constrained.

Furthermore we have to consider the justice of corporate taxation which is based upon profits declared by conventional accounting principles. Yet it has been shown that the *real* profits of most companies will be lower than those conventionally reported*. Such business houses will therefore be paying grossly inflated taxation bills. Furthermore cash flows will be adversely affected by the combination of

1 Increased costs due to inflation — unless the needs for sales price increases are recognised and approved.
2 Payments which do not reflect the true corporate surpluses available for disposal and taxation.

*Current purchasing power accounting enables more favourable earnings ratings to be achieved by companies with high gearing ratios: at the same time those firms with extensive fixed asset investments, financed by a low or nil gearing, will suffer depletion of net incomes: the former group includes property companies, the latter takes in the major engineering companies.

If the taxation of real profits, as against the taxation of money profits, was accomplished then most business managers would be more receptive to inflation accounting. The need for education about the consequences of ignoring the effects of inflation when reporting business wealth and performance is an important need to be met. It concerns business managers, taxation legislators, and trades unions also.

The consequences of accounting for inflation will be evident whatever method is used. This chapter has studied the conversion of historical cost accounts to accounts based upon the general purchasing power of the monetary unit. But other proposals for dealing with inflation in business accounts have been examined and are frequently the subject of debate. Some brief reference must be made therefore to these other suggestions.

The replacement cost method of accounting for fixed assets

The proponents of this method suggest that depreciation charges in the profit and loss account should be based upon costs of replacement of the corporate fixed assets. How that replacement cost is to be determined is not satisfactorily established. In fact replacement cost data would most likely result from estimates made, by management, of the current costs of replacing the fixed assets. Criticisms of this method of accounting for inflation include the following items:

1   Replacement cost estimates would be influenced by the personal opinions of those making the estimates.
2   The system postulates replacement of existing assets by exactly similar items — a somewhat unrealistic assumption.
3   Future changes in the company's product ranges, or its line of business, are not envisaged.
4   Increases in depreciation charges would be effective from the years in which the fixed assets were revalued: but the implied undercharges for depreciation in previous years would not be corrected.
5   No account is taken of the impacts of inflation upon stocks or upon holding monetary items.

Writing up fixed asset values in the balance sheet

This method requires that fixed asset net book values shall be written up to amounts which are deemed to represent their current cost.

Again problems will arise about an appropriate method of determining
these values — personal opinions will intervene. Furthermore current
values of corporate assets will be affected by

> Scarcity, and
> Technological changes

as well as by inflation. Many of the criticisms directed to the replacement cost method, as stated above, will apply to this proposal also.

The current value method

Here the argument is based upon a concept which states that the
value of an output must be measured by the *current* cost of the input
(assets and services) necessary to achieve the output. Thus we would
be involved in determining current costs of stock consumed and in
revising annual depreciation charges to ensure that they matched with
the current costs of the fixed assets involved. Once more the difficulty
of valuation arises: one cannot envisage any such current cost
assessments being entirely free from personal opinion. Criticisms of
fixed asset replacement cost method will apply to the current value
method also.

However, the reader should realise that the current purchasing
power method of accounting for inflation has its critics also. The
main item of criticism refers to our using the Consumer Price Index
as the conversion rating for the accounts of all companies. It is argued
that a replacement cost method is more reliable. In this system
specific *industry* indexes would be used to effect an updating of data
in company accounts, instead of some general index such as the
Consumer Price Index. An example of a specific index would refer
to oil prices: the index of oil prices should be used — it is suggested —
as the conversion factor for those firms engaged in the oil business,
or those which use large quantities of oil products in their manufacturing processes. The system would be a complex one with many
separate indexes being necessary for the complete application of
inflation accounting throughout industry. Yet it has to be admitted
that specific indexes for the principal input items in the operations
of any business, could be compiled. With stocks of materials, replacement purchase prices could be readily ascertained for the
purposes of our replacement cost index. The same could not be said
for fixed assets. These change in design, performance and cost. It may
well be that it would not be possible or advisable to replace an asset
by something exactly the same.

The problem can be settled when the objectives of preparing final
accounts are unequivocally specified. When we use a consumer price

index we recognise that we are concerning ourselves with the purchasing power of the average consumer. To apply this index in our conversion processes implies an aim of preserving the purchasing power of those who invest in industrial ventures, i.e. the general body of shareholders. To use a specific industrial index implies an aim of preserving the purchasing power of firms, or at least of their special groups of investors.

But the objectives of preparing final accounts cannot be so simply defined. We have to rationalise our striving for a more realistic reporting of corporate wealth and profitability. So far as profitability is concerned, we need to know in real terms whether a business consumes goods and services efficiently and economically, in producing its output. Profits, as quantified in the accounts, will have a material influence upon the level of dividend payments and the ultimate Corporation Tax computations — both of these items resulting in cash outflows. Now in past years, high accounting profits accompanied by high annual dividends have always had an impact upon the market value of a company's ordinary shares. They have tended to stimulate a higher rather than a lower share price, relative to the market as a whole. Yet *during a period of inflation*, the presence of high profits does not necessarily mean that there will be a sufficiency of liquid resources to pay

> Creditors
> Dividends
> Taxation, and
> Maintain or improve the firm's physical assets

so that it can continue to generate the same level of business as previously. If these requirements cannot be accomplished the firm will lose credit worthiness: its standing in the market will fall and despite its reported accounting profits, the firm may be worthless. The situation arises because the cost of replacement of fixed assets and stocks will, due to a high rate of inflation, absorb all of the profit cash flow and more besides.

Current purchasing power accounting has been designed to overcome the deficiencies of conventional historical cost reporting: it will go some way towards remedying the misleading contents of conventional accounting, as has been shown in this chapter. But current purchasing power accounting is a backward looking concept: it treats the *past* costs of business activity in the conversion processes. In an inflationary environment, it is the future levels of business costs which are more relevant to an appraisal of business worth as well as for business survival. The costs of acquiring and replacing corporate assets at various times in the future will be vital factors affecting the power of a firm to remain in business, or at least to maintain its present level of business activity. The supporters of replacement cost accounting stress these matters in their opposition to the adoption of current purchasing power accounting. Clearly the use of a general index of purchasing power cannot reflect the impact of inflation upon the replacement costs of all business. Some commodities and assets, used in specific industries, will move against the general trend of prices and could be acquired more cheaply than in the past. Current purchasing power accounting would — by the application of a general index of purchasing power — recognise the reductions in replacement cost as a profit. The actual cost of replacement of the lower priced assets would not be reflected in the conversion (of past costs) processes of current purchasing power accounting. Therefore the sophistication of current purchasing power accounting may itself produce misleading information for some managements and shareholders. The question of the objectives of preparing final accounts is relevant to the whole debate, but this question has not yet been answered satisfactorily.

Further reading

P. Bird, *Accountability: standards in financial reporting*, Accountancy Age Books (1973).

R. S. Gynther, *Accounting for price-level changes: theory, and procedures*, Pergamon Press (1966).

L.A. Wilk, *Accounting for inflation*, Sweet & Maxwell (1960).

P.R.A. Kirkman, *Accounting under inflationary conditions*, George Allen & Unwin (1974).

A.M. Bourn (Editor), *Studies in accounting for management decision*, McGraw-Hill (1969). (See especially Chapters 3-5).

D. Bawtry, 'How inflation erodes income,' *The Accountant*, pp 587-82 (4 May 1972).

H.H. Schofield *et al.*, 'The effects of inflation on investment appraisal', *Journal of Business Finance* (Summer 1973).

B.A. Lietner, 'Prepare your company for inflation', *Harvard Business Review*, pp 113-25 (September/October, 1970).

R.S. Cutler and C.A. Westwick, 'The impact of inflation on share values', *Accountancy*, p 15 *et seq.* (March 1973).

6 | *Disclosure of information*

Introduction

The principal enactments governing the activities of UK limited companies are the 1948 and 1967 Companies Acts. Also certain proposed changes in, and additions to, the provisions of these enactments were detailed in a Companies Bill. Therefore to further our studies of corporate finance we shall now examine

1 The extent to which companies are compelled, by the above enactments, to disclose information about their activities, and
2 The possible future developments in the disclosure requirements of public limited companies.

The 1948 Act (section 158) and the 1967 Act (section 24) state that a copy of the annual report of the directors, the balance sheet and its attached profit and loss account, together with a copy of the auditors' report shall be sent to

1 Every member of the company.
2 Every holder of debentures in the company.
3 All other entitled persons.

Now the reader has studied the form and content of published balance sheets and profit and loss accounts, in earlier chapters. But the totality of corporate information which companies are required to disclose is not accomplished in the published accounts only. The annual report of the directors is also a major vehicle for issuing specified information to all interested parties.

Section 157 of the 1948 Act requires that a 'report by the directors with respect to the state of the company's affairs, the amount if any which they recommend should be paid by way of dividend, and the amount if any which they propose to carry to reserves . . .' shall accompany any balance sheet which is laid before the company at its annual general meeting. The spirit of much of these legal requirements shows that past company legislation has been directed mainly to the interests of shareholders and creditors of the company. There are no legal directives compelling firms to have regard to the public interest, or to the special interests of its employees*. However this does not mean that company managements have not concerned themselves with these issues. The Chairman of ICI Limited in his foreword to the 1973 Report and Accounts said

'. . . ICI has always considered itself accountable not only to stockholders, but also to a wide range of other interests — including the public at large . . .'

Again the Chairman of the Rockware Group Limited, in his statement which accompanied the 1971 accounts, referred at length to environmental problems and the waste of natural resources, and the way his company has addressed itself to these matters.

The directors' report

The meagre requirements regarding the content of the directors' report as originally set out in the 1948 Act, were enlarged considerably by the 1967 Act. Additional information which must now be given in the directors' report, in consequence of the 1967 Act, is given below

1   The names of persons who at any time during the financial year were directors of the company. [Section 16(1)]
2   The principal activities of the company and its subsidiaries during that year, and any significant changes in those activities during the year [Section 16(1)]

---

*Certain special acts which could be said to encompass the term 'public interest' do exist of course. These include Weights & Measures Acts, the Trade Descriptions Acts and the Fair Trading Act. But the writer gives a wider meaning to 'public interest', in the above paragraph, than these special acts would convey.

3   Details of any significant changes, which have occurred during the year, in the fixed assets of the company or of its subsidiaries: furthermore if the market value of land at the year end differs substantially from its book value as given in the balance sheet, an indication of the significance of the difference if any must be given. [Section 16(1)a]

4   Where shares or debentures were issued during the year, a statement of the reasons for the issue(s) must be given together with details of the class of shares or debentures issued and the amounts received from each issue. [Section 16(1)b]

5   Details must be given of contracts between the company and any of its directors (other than contracts of service), or any contract with the company in which a director has an interest either directly or indirectly: the information must show the
    names of the parties to the contract
    name(s) of the director(s) — if not a party to the contract
    nature of the contract and the nature of the director's interest [Section 16(1)c]

6   Where arrangements exist at the end of the year between the company and its directors to enable directors to acquire benefits by the acquisition of shares or debentures in the company, or any other company, the report shall explain the arrangements giving details of the directors involved: the same requirements apply to any similar arrangement which existed *during the year*. [Section 16(1)d]

7   Details of directors' interests in the shares or debentures of the company, of every subsidiary or holding company: the information given must state the position at the beginning and at the end of the year. [Section 16(1)e]

8   In addition to the requirements noted in (1) to (7) above the report must give particulars of any other matters which would be necessary for an appreciation of the state of the company's affairs provided that, in the opinion of the directors, it would not be harmful to the company and its subsidiaries for such information to be disclosed. [Section 16(1)f]

9   Where the company carries on business of two or more distinct classes (other than banking or discounting) which differ substantially from each other, a statement shall be made of turnover and profit or loss (pretax) of each class. [Section 17]

10   There must be a statement of the average number of persons employed in each week in the year by the company, and its subsidiaries if any, and the aggregate remuneration paid or payable for the year to the persons by reference to whom the above average number was ascertained.

This requirement does not extend to companies with less than 100 employees or the companies which are wholly owned subsidiaries of another UK company. [Section 18]

11   If the company gives money for political and/or charitable purposes and if the sums involved exceed £50, the directors' report shall specify

    (a)   the name of the person to whom the money has been given and the amount involved:

    (b)   the political party to whom the money has been given and the amount involved.

Again these provisions do not apply to companies which are wholly owned subsidiaries of another UK company. In the case of a holding company and its subsidiaries the statement shall refer to their aggregate contributions. [Section 19]

12   If the company's turnover exceeds £50,000, there shall be disclosed

    (a)   a statement of the value of the exports during the year

    (b)   if no goods were exported during the year, a statement to that effect.

For a holding company and its subsidiaries, similar information must be given for the group provided that the group's turnover exceeds £50,000. [Section 20]

In those cases where the above information is *not* disclosed in the accounts but is included in the directors' report, then the corresponding amounts for the immediately preceding financial year — for the item involved — shall be given.

We have to appreciate that the main purpose of the directors' report is to give shareholders and others a commentary on the state of affairs of the business. The commentary is related mostly to matters impacting upon the balance sheet and accounts which are presented at a general meeting of the company. To this end the statutory disclosure requirements noted on pages 179 to 192 ensure that a minimum of relevant information is given, when the accounts are published. But if some event of material significance for the company's fortunes had arisen since the date of the balance sheet then details of that event should be recorded in the report. It may well be that the consequences of the post-balance sheet event had not (quite properly) been brought to account in the accounting statements laid before the company's general meeting.

The directors have some discretion. They are allowed to use that discretion by not disclosing items which they consider would be harmful to the business (item 8, page 176). Again they are required to use their judgement, in certain cases, as to what ought to be disclosed. Here the reporting of significant variations between the book and market values of land, the analyses of turnover and pre-tax profits for the principal classes of business which the firm undertakes, are cases in point. Clearly there can be no universal specification as to what is significant in land value variations, or how incomes and costs are to be allocated for the analysis of pre-tax profits. But the directors should produce a report which, together with the balance sheet and accounts, will facilitate a reasoned appraisal, by members of the company, of the state of affairs of the company.

The future

It is not expected that the disclosure requirements relating to directors' reports will be any less rigorous, in the future, than those outlined above. On the contrary, there are clear indications that the information to be reported will grow in both nature and content. Many of these new requirements will relate to the firm's work-force and could include publication of the firm's

> Employee turnover rate
> Employee redundancies
> Industrial relations policies
> Industrial health and safety record
> Manpower planning

An adequate reporting of the financial state of a company's affairs must also demand that Funds Flow Statements — in meaningful form — be included in the annual report and accounts booklets and laid before the members in general meeting. Furthermore the publication of data on corporate research and development expenditure and on specific plans for capital expenditure may well be requirements. However subjects such as these could be areas where the directors' discretion could be allowed to operate.

The annual accounts

The Second Schedule to *The Companies Act, 1967,* contains detailed provisions regarding the information to be reported by companies, in or in notes accompanying the balance sheets and profit and loss accounts being laid before the members in a general meeting. These detailed specifications are reproduced below by kind permission of Her Majesty's Stationery Office. The presentation does not follow the precise layout and sequence of items in the Act, because here matters of related interest are brought together under appropriately descriptive sub-headings.

The first group of disclosure provisions concerns balance sheet data. Now it does not follow that all of the requirements can be satisfied only by specific entries in the format of the balance sheet itself. Such rigidity could lead to unwieldy documents containing potentially incomprehensible masses of words and figures. This would defeat the objectives of disclosure. Thus we find that certain of the sections of the Second Schedule prescribed alternate ways of giving information —

> 'Para. 7. There shall also be shown *(unless it is shown in the profit and loss account or a statement or report annexed thereto . . .) [Author's italics]*

Furthermore all of the requirements of paragraph 11 to the Second Schedule '. . . shall be stated by way of note, or in a statement or report annexed (to the balance sheet) if not otherwise shown . . .' With these comments in mind the reader can proceed to study the detailed wording of the disclosure requirements embodied in the 1948 and 1967 Companies Acts.

BALANCE SHEET INFORMATION

Capital

(a) Share capital: redemption of preference shares: share premium account: redeemable debentures.

The authorised share capital, issue share capital, liabilities and assets shall be summarised, with such particulars as are necessary to disclose the general nature of the assets and liabilities, and there shall be specified -

(a) any part of the issued capital that consists of redeemable preference shares, the earliest and latest dates on which the company has power to redeem those shares, whether those must be redeemed in any event or are liable to be redeemed at the option of the company and whether any (and, if so, what) premium is payable in redemption;

(b) so far as the information is not given in the profit and loss account, any share capital on which interest has been paid out of capital during the financial year, and the rate at which interest has been so paid;

(c) the amount of the share premium account;

(d) particulars of any redeemed debentures which the company has power to reissue.

[para. 2]

(b) Debentures held by trustee for, or nominee of, the company.

Where any of the company's debentures are held by a nominee of or trustee for the company, the nominal amount of the debentures and the amount at which they are stated in the books of the company shall be stated.

[para. 10]

(c) Option to subscribe for the company's shares.

The number, description and amount of any shares in the company which any person has an option to subscribe for, together with the following particulars of the option, that is to say -

(a) the period during which it is exercisable;

(b) the price to be paid for shares subscribed for under it.

[para. 11(2)]

(d) Arrears of fixed cumulative dividends.

The amount of any arrears of fixed cumulative dividends on the company's shares and the period for which the dividends or, if there is more than one class, each class of them are in arrear, the amount to be stated before deduction of income tax, except that, in the case of tax free dividends, the amount shall be shown free of tax and the fact that it is so shown shall also be stated.

[para. 11(3)]

Capital formation and issue expenses

There shall be stated under separate headings, so far as they are not written off -

(a) the preliminary expenses;

(b) any expenses incurred in connection with any issue of share capital or debentures;

(c) any sums paid by way of commission in respect of any shares or debentures;

(d) any sums allowed by way of discount in respect of any debentures; and

(e) the amount of the discount allowed on any issue of shares at a discount.

[para. 3]

(a) Disclosure of amounts.

The aggregate amounts respectively of reserves and provisions (other than provisions for depreciation, renewals or diminution in value of assets) shall be stated under separate headings:
Provided that -

(a) this paragraph shall not require a separate statement of either of the said amounts which is not material; and

(b) the Board of Trade may direct that it shall not require a separate statement of the amount of provisions where they are satisfied that that is not required in the public interest and would prejudice the company, but subject to the condition that any heading stating an amount arrived at after taking into account a provision (other than as aforesaid) shall be so framed or marked as to indicate that fact.

[para. 6]

(b) Transfers to and from.

There shall also be shown (unless it is shown in the profit and loss account or a statement or report annexed thereto, or the amount involved is not material) -

(a) where the amount of the reserves or of the provisions (other than provisions for depreciation, renewals or diminution in value of assets) shows an increase as compared with the amount at the end of the immediately preceding financial year, the source from which the amount of the increase had been derived; and

(b) where -

(i) the amount of the reserves shows a decrease as compared with the amount at the end of the immediately preceding financial year; or

(ii) the amount at the end of the immediately preceding financial year of the provisions (other than provisions for depreciation, renewals or diminution in value of assets) exceeded the aggregate of the sums since applied and amounts still retained for the purposes thereof;

the application of the amounts derived from the difference.

[para. 7(1)]

(a) Reserves, provisions, liabilities and assets.
The reserves, provisions, liabilities and assets shall be classified under headings appropriate to the company's business:
Provided that -
(a) where the amount of any class is not material, it may be included under the same heading as some other class; and
(b) where any assets of one class are not separable from assets of another class, those assets may be included under the same heading.
Fixed assets, current assets and assets that are neither fixed nor current shall be separately identified.

[para. 4 (1) & (2)]

(b) Investments, loans, overdrafts, goodwill, patents, trademarks.
There shall be shown under separate headings -
(a) the aggregate amounts respectively of the company's quoted investments and unquoted investments;
(b) if the amount of the goodwill and of any patents and trade marks or part of that amount is shown as a separate item in or is otherwise ascertainable from the books of the company, or from any contract for the sale or purchase of any property to be acquired by the company, or from any documents in the possession of the company relating to the stamp duty payable in respect of any such contract or the conveyance of any such property, the said amount so shown or ascertained so far as not written off or, as the case may be, the said amount so far as it is so shown or ascertainable and as so shown or ascertained, as the case may be;
(c) the aggregate amount of any outstanding loans made under the authority of provisos (b) and (c) of subsection (1) of section fifty-four of the 1948 Act, i.e. loans to enable purchase of the company's own shares;
(d) the aggregate amount of bank loans and overdrafts and the aggregate amount of loans made to the company which -
(i) are repayable otherwise than by instalments and fall due for repayment after the expiration of the period of five years beginning with the day next following the expiration of the financial year; or
(ii) are repayable by instalments any of which fall due for payment after the expiration of that period;
not being, in either case, bank loans or overdrafts;

Nothing in head (b) of the foregoing sub-paragraph shall be taken as requiring the amount of the goodwill, patents and trade marks to be stated otherwise than as a single item.

[para. 8(1) & (2)]

Assets

(a) (1) Book values of fixed assets.

The method of arriving at the amount of any fixed asset shall, subject to the next following sub-paragraph, be to take the difference between -

(a)   its cost or, if it stands in the company's books at a valuation, the amount of the valuation; and

(b)   the aggregate amount provided or written off since the date of acquisition or valuation, as the case may be, for depreciation or diminution in value;

and for the purposes of this paragraph the net amount at which any assets stand in the company's books at the commencement of this Act (after deduction of the amounts previously provided or written off for depreciation or diminution in value) shall, if the figures relating to the period before the commencement of this [1948] Act cannot be obtained without unreasonable expense or delay, be treated as if it were the amount of a valuation of those assets made at the commencement of this [1948] Act and, where any of those assets are sold, the said net amount less the amount of the sales shall be treated as if it were the amount of a valuation so made of the remaining assets.

(2) The foregoing sub-paragraph shall not apply -

(a)   to assets for which the figures relating to the period beginning with the commencement of this Act cannot be obtained without unreasonable expense or delay; or

(b)   to assets the replacement of which is provided for wholly or partly -

(i)   by making provision for renewals and charging the cost of replacement against the provision so made; or

(ii)   by charging the cost of replacement direct to revenue; or

(c)   to any quoted investments or to any unquoted investments or to any unquoted investments of which the value as estimated by the directors is shown either as the amount of the investments or by way of note; or

(d)   to goodwill, patents or trade marks.

For the assets under each heading whose amount is arrived at in accordance with sub-paragraph (1) of this paragraph, there shall be shown -

(a) the aggregate of the amounts referred to in paragraph (a) of that sub-paragraph; and

(b) the aggregate of the amounts referred to in paragraph (b) thereof.

As respects the assets under each heading whose amount is not arrived at in accordance with the said sub-paragraph (1) because their replacement is provided for as mentioned in sub-paragraph (2) (b) of this paragraph, there shall be stated -

(a) the means by which their replacement is provided for; and

(b) the aggregate amount of the provision (if any) made for renewals and not used.

[para. 5(1), (2), (3) & (4)]

The method or methods used to arrive at the amount of the fixed assets under each heading shall be stated.

[para. 4(3)]

(b) Charges on fixed assets.

Where any liability of the company is secured otherwise than by operation of law on any assets of the company, the fact that that liability is so secured shall be stated, but it shall not be necessary to specify the assets on which the liability is secured.

[para. 9]

Particulars of any charge on the assets of the company to secure the liabilities of any other person, including, where practicable, the amount secured.

[para. 11(4)]

(c) Fixed asset acquisitions and disposals.

If there are included amongst fixed assets under any heading (other than investments) assets that have been acquired during the financial year, the aggregate amount of the assets acquired as determined for the purpose of making up the balance sheet, and if during that year any fixed assets included under a heading in the balance sheet made up with respect to the immediately preceding financial year (other than investments) have been disposed of or destroyed, the aggregate amount thereof as determined for the purpose of making up that balance sheet.

[para. 11(6B)]

(d) Valuation of fixed assets.

In the case of fixed assets under any heading whose amount is required to be arrived at in accordance with paragraph 5(1) of this Schedule (other than unquoted investments) and is so arrived at by reference to a valuation, the years (so far as they are known to the directors) in which the assets were severally valued and the several values, and, in the case of assets that have been valued during the financial year, the names of the persons who valued them or particulars of their qualifications for doing so and (whichever is stated) the bases of valuation used by them.

[para. 11(6A)]

(e) Freehold and leasehold land.

Of the amount of fixed assets consisting of land, how much is ascribable to land of freehold tenure and how much to land of leasehold tenure, and, of the latter, how much is ascribed to land held on long lease and how much land held on short lease.

[para. 11(6C)]

(f) Values of current assets.

If in the opinion of the directors any of the current assets have not a value, on realisation in the ordinary course of the company's business, at least equal to the amount at which they are stated, the fact that the directors are of that opinion.

[para. 11(7)]

(g) Value of stock or work in progress.

If the amount carried forward for stock in trade or work in progress is material for the appreciation by its members of the company's state of affairs or of its profit or loss for the financial year, the manner in which that amount has been computed.

[para. 11(8B)]

Investments

(a) Classification.

There shall be shown under separate headings -
(a)   the aggregate amounts respectively of the company's quoted investments and unquoted investments;

[para. 8(1a)]

The heading showing the amount of the quoted investments

shall be subdivided, where necessary, to distinguish the investments as respects which there has, and those as respects which there has not, been granted a quotation or permission to deal on a recognised stock exchange.

[para. 8(3)]

(b) Quoted investments.

The aggregate market value of the company's quoted investments where it differs from the amount of the investments as stated, and the stock exchange value of any investments of which the market value is shown (whether separately or not) and is taken as being higher than their stock exchange value.

[para. 11(8)]

(c) Unquoted investments.

In the case of unquoted investments consisting in equity share capital of other bodies corporate (*other than any whose values as estimated by the directors are separately shown*), the matters referred to in the following heads shall, if not otherwise shown, be stated by way of note or in a statement or report annexed:-

(a)   the aggregate amount of the company's income for the financial year that is ascribed to the investments;

(b)   the amount of the company's share before taxation, and the amount of that share after taxation, of the net aggregate amount of the profits of the bodies in which the investments are held, being profits for the several periods to which accounts sent by them during the financial year to the company related, after deducting those bodies' losses for those periods (or vice versa);

(c)   the amount of the company's share of the net aggregate amount of the undistributed profits accumulated by the bodies in which the investments are held since the time when the investments were acquired, after deducting the losses accumulated by them since that time (or vice versa);

(d)   the manner in which any losses incurred by the said bodies have been dealt with in the company's accounts.

[para. 5A]

Miscellaneous

(a) Taxation.

If a reserve or provision is set aside for the purpose of its being used to prevent undue fluctuations in charges for taxation, it shall be stated.

[para. 7A]

If a sum set aside for the purpose of its being used to prevent undue fluctuations in charges for taxation has been used during the financial year for another purpose, the amount thereof and the fact that it has been so used.

[para. 11(8A)]

The basis on which the amount, if any, set aside for United Kingdom corporation tax is computed.

[para. 11(10)]

(b) Contingent liability.
The general nature of any other contingent liabilities not provided for and, where practicable, the aggregate amount or estimated amount of those liabilities, if it is material.

[para. 11(5)]

(c) Capital expenditure contracts.
Where practicable the aggregate amount or estimated amount if it is material, of contracts for capital expenditure, so far as not provided for and, where practicable, the aggregate amount or estimated amount, if it is material, of capital expenditure authorised by the directors which has not been contracted for.

[para. 11(6)]

(d) Foreign currency conversion.
The basis on which foreign currencies have been converted into sterling, where the amount of the assets or liabilities affected is material.

[para. 11(9)]

(e) Prior year's figures.
Except in the case of the first balance sheet laid before the company before the commencement of this Act, the corresponding amounts at the end of the immediately preceding financial year for all items shown in the balance sheet.

[para. 11(11)]

PROFIT AND LOSS ACCOUNT INFORMATION

Annual turnover

1   The matters referred to below shall be stated by way of note, if not otherwise shown.

2   The turnover for the financial year, except in so far as it is attributable to the business of banking or discounting or to business of such other class as may be prescribed for the purposes of this sub-paragraph.

3   If some or all of the turnover is omitted by reason of its being attributable as aforesaid, the fact that it is so omitted.

4   The method by which turnover is arrived at.

5   A company shall not be subject to the requirements of this paragraph if it is neither a holding company nor a subsidiary of another body corporate and the turnover which, apart from this sub-paragraph, would be required to be stated does not exceed £5,000.

[para. 13A]

Depreciation

There shall be shown -
(a)   the amount charged to revenue by way of provision for depreciation, renewals or diminution in value of fixed assets;

[para. 12(1) (a)]

If, in the case of any assets in whose case an amount is charged to revenue by way of provision for depreciation or diminution in value, an amount is also charged by way of provision for renewal thereof, the last-mentioned amount shall be shown separately.

[para. 12(3)]

If the amount charged to revenue by way of provision for depreciation or diminution in value of any fixed assets (other than investments) has been determined otherwise than by reference to the amount of those assets as determined for the purpose of making up the balance sheet, that fact shall be stated.

[para. 12(4)]

If depreciation or replacement of fixed assets is provided for by some method other than a depreciation charge or provision for renewals, or is not provided for, the method by which it is provided for or the fact that it is not provided for, as the case may be.

[para. 14(2)]

Interest on loans etc.

There shall be shown -
the amount of the interest on loans of the following kinds made

to the company (whether on the security of debentures or not), namely, bank loans, overdrafts and loans which, not being bank loans or overdrafts, -

(i)   are repayable otherwise than by instalments and fall due for repayment before the expiration of the period of five years beginning with the day following the expiration of the financial year; or

(ii)   are repayable by instalments the last of which falls due for payment before the expiration of that period;

and the amount of the interest on loans of other kinds so made (whether on the security of debentures or not);

[para. 12(1)(b)]

Reserves and provisions

There shall be shown -

the amount, if material, set aside or proposed to be set aside to, or withdrawn from, reserves;

[para. 12(1)(e)]

There shall be shown -

subject to sub-paragraph (2) of this paragraph, the amount, if material, set aside to provisions other than provisions for depreciation, renewals or diminution in value of assets or, as the case may be, the amount, if material, withdrawn from such provisions and not applied for the purposes thereof;

[para. 12(1)(f)]

The Board of Trade may direct that a company shall not be obliged to show an amount set aside to provisions in accordance with sub-paragraph (1)(f), if the Board is satisfied that that is not required in the public interest and would prejudice the company, but subject to the condition that any heading stating an amount arrived at after taking into account the amount set aside as aforesaid shall be so framed or marked as to indicate that fact.

[para. 12(2)]

Redemption of capital

There shall be shown -

the amounts respectively provided for redemption of share capital and for redemption of loans;

[para. 12(1)(d)]

There shall be shown -
> the amount, if material, charged to revenue in respect of sums payable in respect of the hire of plant and machinery;

[para. 12(1)(gb)]

Auditors' remuneration

The amount of the remuneration of the auditors shall be shown under a separate heading, and for the purposes of this paragraph, any sums paid by the company in respect of the auditors' expenses shall be deemed to be included in the expression 'remuneration'.

[para. 13]

Taxation

There shall be shown -
> the amount of the charge to revenue for United Kingdom corporation tax and, if that amount would have been greater but for relief from double taxation, the amount which it would have been but for such relief, the amount of the charge for United Kingdom income tax and the amount for the charge for taxation imposed outside the United Kingdom of profits, income and (so far as charged to revenue) capital gains;

[para. 12(1)(c)]

The basis on which the charge for United Kingdom corporation tax and United Kingdom tax is computed.

[para. 14(3)]

Any special circumstances which affect liability in respect of taxation of profits, income or capital gains for the financial year or liability in respect of taxation of profits, income or capital gains for succeeding financial years.

[para. 14(3A)]

Investment income

There shall be shown -
> the amounts respectively of income from quoted investments

and income from unquoted investments;

[para. 12(1)(g)]

Rent income

There shall be shown -
    if a substantial part of the company's revenue for the financial
year consists of rents from land, the amount thereof (after
deduction of ground-rents, rates and other out-goings);

[para. 12(1)(ga)]

Dividends

There shall be shown -
    the aggregate amount (before deduction of income tax) of the
dividends paid and proposed.

[para. 12(1)(h)]

Prior year

The amount of any charge arising in consequence of the occurrence
of an event in a preceding financial year and of any credit so arising
shall, be stated under a separate heading, if it is not included in a
heading related to other matters.

[para. 12A]

Except in the case of the first profit and loss account laid before the
company after the commencement of this Act the corresponding
amounts for the immediately preceding financial year for all items
shown in the profit and loss account. (To be stated by way of note,
if not otherwise shown).

[para. 14(5)]

Unusual items

Any material respects in which items shown in the profit and loss
account are affected -
(a)   by transactions of a sort not usually undertaken by the company
    or otherwise by circumstances of an exceptional or non-
    recurrent nature; or

(b) by any change in the basis of accounting.
(to be stated by way of note, if not otherwise shown).

[para. 14(6)]

Further reading

F.H. Jones, *Guide to company balance sheets and profit and loss accounts,* W. Heffer and Sons, Cambridge (Sixth Edition, 1964).

R.W. Wallis, *Accounting: a modern approach,* McGraw-Hill (1970). (See especially Chapters 13 and 17-20).

'Disclosure of accounting policies,' *Accountant,* pp 117-9 (28 January 1971).

Glossary of Common Accounting and Financial Terms

Certain items in this glossary have been taken from the Management-Development Programme operated by General Foods Limited, Banbury, Oxon. The author gratefully acknowledges the permission, given by the appropriate official of the company, to reproduce some of the items used in that Programme. Terminology has been amended to recognise UK customs and statutes.

Five items (marked *) are quoted from publications of the Institute of Chartered Accountants in England and Wales. Due thanks and acknowledgement are here made by the author for the permission, given by the Institute's appropriate officer, for publication of the extracts. Their inclusion in the glossary has been deemed relevant by decision of the author.

Amortisation   A reduction in a debt or fund by periodic payments covering interest and part of the principal: also a charge against earnings to write off the cost of an intangible asset over a period of years.

Assets   Everything a business owns or is due to it: *current assets,* such as cash, short-term deposits, debtors, stocks of raw materials, work-in-progress and finished goods; *fixed assets,* such as buildings and machinery; and *intangible assets,* such as patents and good will.

Balance sheet   A statement showing the nature and amount of a company's assets, liabilities, and capital on a given date. In money terms, the balance sheet shows what the company owned, what it owed, and the ownership interest in the company of its shareholders. A *consolidated balance sheet* is one showing the financial condition of a holding or parent company and its subsidiaries. A *narrative balance sheet* is one which is written in vertical — rather than two sided — form.

*Basic accounts   those prepared substantially in accordance with established conventions on the basis of historical cost and include those in which some or all of the fixed assets have been revalued and/or some or all current assets are shown at estimated realisable value.

Bond or Debenture   A written promise to pay the holder a sum of money at a certain time (more than one year after issue) at a stated annual rate of interest. Debentures are frequently secured on the assets of the company. Where not secured they are termed 'naked' debentures.

Book value   The book value of an ordinary share is determined from a company's records, by adding all assets (generally excluding such intangibles as good will), then deducting all debts and other liabilities, plus the liquidation price of any preference shares. The sum arrived at is divided by the *number* of ordinary shares outstanding and the result is the book value per share. Book value of the assets of a company or a security may have little or no significant relationship to market value. The book value of an ordinary share is also termed the 'net asset value' of the share.

Capitalisation   Total amount of the various securities issued by a company. Capitalisation may include loan stock, preference and ordinary shares. They are usually shown in the books of the issuing company at their nominal or face value.

Cash flow   Reported net income of a company plus non-cash charges such as depreciation and charges to reserves (which are bookkeeping deductions and not paid out in cash). Other terms such as gross cash flow and net cash flow are derived from the pre- and post-tax net incomes plus non-cash charges.

Collateral   Securities or other property pledged by a borrower to secure repayment of a loan.

*Conversion   The process of translating figures from historical pounds to pounds of current purchasing power.

Convertible   A debenture, that may be exchanged by the owner for ordinary shares or another security of the same company, in accordance with the terms of the issue.

Current assets   Those assets of a company that are reasonably expected to be realised in cash, or sold, or consumed during the normal operating cycle of the business. These include cash, debtors, short-term investments, and all forms of stock. Frequently called *circulating assets* because they are (or should be) constantly on the move being converted, in the production and marketing process, from raw material stock to cash (received from sales).

Current liabilities   Money owed and payable by a company, usually within the normal operating cycle of the business. Items due and payable within one year may also be classified as current liabilities.

Depreciation   Charges against earnings to write off the cost, less salvage value, of a fixed asset over its estimated useful life. It is a book-keeping entry and does not represent any cash outlay, nor are any funds earmarked for the purpose.

Dividend   The payment recommended by the board of directors to be distributed to shareholders. On Preference shares, it is generally a fixed percentage of the share's nominal value. On Ordinary shares, the dividend varies with the fortunes of the company and the amount of cash on hand, and may be omitted at the discretion of the directors if business is poor or if they determine to withhold earnings to invest in plant and equipment, research and development, and so on. Sometimes a company will pay a dividend out of past earnings even if it is not currently operating at a profit. The proposed rate of dividend on Ordinary shares must be approved by the members in general meeting, before it is paid.

Equity   The ownership interest of ordinary shareholders in a company.

Fixed charges A class of business expense which cannot be identified with a specific output, except by some kind of subjective allocation. These expenses do not generally vary in money size as production varies and most fixed expenses will continue even if production were discontinued.

Investments When appearing on a balance sheet, this term represents the investment in another company. The value shown is usually the original cost of the investment. The Companies Acts require balance sheet entries to show investments in two main groups — quoted investments and unquoted investments.

Liabilities All the claims against a company. Liabilities include accounts and wages and salaries payable, dividends declared payable, accrued taxes payable, and fixed or long-term liabilities, such as mortgage bonds, debentures, and bank loans.

Minority interests In consolidated balance sheets, this term describes the liability of the group towards the minority shareholders being that part of the total assets and earnings due to them. This arises where, for example, the accounts of a less than 100%-owned subsidiary are consolidated and shown in the group accounts: 100% of the subsidiary assets are consolidated in the group accounts; the fraction of assets belonging to the minority shareholders in the subsidiary are shown as a liability of the group.

*Monetary items Assets, liabilities or capital, the amounts of which are fixed by contract or statute in terms of the numbers of pounds regardless of changes in the purchasing power of the pound.

Mortgage debenture A bond secured by a mortgage on a property. The value of the property may or may not equal the value of the bonds issued against it.

Net worth Total assets less amounts due creditors. It includes both issued shares and reserves: also called total shareholders' interest.

*Non-monetary items All items which are not monetary items, with the exception of total equity interest, i.e. share capital, reserves and retained profits. The total equity interest is neither a monetary nor a non-monetary item.

Ordinary shares: The ownership interest in a limited company. If the company has also issued Preference shares, both Ordinary and

Preference have ownership rights. However, the preferred normally has prior claim on dividends and, in the event of liquidation, on assets as well. Claims of both ordinary and preference shareholders are junior to claims of debenture holders and other creditors of the company. Ordinary shareholders assume the greater risk, but generally exercise the greater control and may gain the greater reward in the form of dividends and capital appreciation.

Preference share   A class of share with a claim on the company's earnings, at a specified rate, before payment may be made to the Ordinary shareholders. Also usually entitled to priority over Ordinary shareholders if the company liquidates. *Cumulative preference shares* have a provision that if one or more dividends are omitted, the omitted dividends must be paid before dividends may be paid on the company's Ordinary shares.

Profit and loss statement or income statement   A statement summarising the income and expenditure of a company to show net profit or loss for the period involved.

Sinking fund   Money regularly set aside by a company to redeem its loan stock or preference shares from time to time. A sinking fund may also be used to make provisions for fixed asset replacement.

Share dividend   A dividend paid in shares rather than cash. The dividend is usually additional shares of the issuing company.

Surplus   The excess of assets over liabilities and issued shares. When accumulated from profits, it is called retained earnings and may be shown — in part — as a general reserve. If from other sources, it is called capital surplus. The sale of shares at prices above the nominal value result in a premium equal to the excess of sale price over nominal value. This premium is shown in the balance sheet as a 'share premium account' — a form of capital surplus.

*Updating   The process of translating figures of an earlier accounting period from pounds of current purchasing power at one date to pounds of current purchasing power at another, later date.

Working capital   The difference between current assets and current liabilities.

Yield   Also known as return. The dividends or interest paid by a company expressed as a percentage of the current market price of the shares or debentures involved.

Index